Modern Traction
Rail Mishaps

A pictorial study of accidents, derailments and collisions

Modern Traction
Rail Mishaps

A pictorial study of accidents, derailments and collisions

Compiled by Colin J. Marsden & Christopher G. Perkins

TheRailwayCentre.Com
Publishing

First published 2011

ISBN 978-0-9557887-4-1

© The Railway Centre.Com Ltd

PO Box 45, Dawlish, Devon. EX7 9XY

Code: 01/11/C

Visit The Railway Centre.Com website at www.therailwaycentre.com

Front Cover Top: *Taunton Fairwater Yard saw a major derailment on 28 March 2009, when a set of points on the reception road split under a moving train. As the wagons tried to travel in different directions over pointwork, three became derailed, with one of the trains YJA wagons turning over onto its side with both bogies ripped off. Recovery was a difficult operation and eventually the Wigan and Margam based cranes undertook recovery overnight on Saturday and Sunday 4/5 April. This was the scene with the two 75 tonne cranes reaching over the stricken wagon.* **Brian Garrett**

Front Cover Bottom: *In the autumn of 1978, Class 37/0 No. 37160 was running light loco off the Shireoaks line towards Doncaster Decoy via the curve at St Catherine's, when for some reason the train passed the signal protecting the junction at danger and went through a pair of catch points. The loco then toppled down the embankment and ended up on its side. Recovery was a complex operation requiring the use of two rail cranes, which lifted the damaged loco once ground stablisation had been undertaken. The loco was then taken to BREL Doncaster Works for repair.* **Derek Porter**

Back Cover Top: *BR Type 2, later Class 24 No. 5028 had charge of 38 wagons forming the 19.30 Ellesmere Port to Mold Junction via Helsby where it reversed on the evening of 9 May 1972. The first five vehicles of the train were tank wagons containing petrol, gas oil and kerosene, after the run round the vacuum pipe was not connected between loco and train. Approaching Chester, on a falling gradient of 1:100 at about 20.50, the driver applied the brakes but found he had insufficient brake power to stop his train. It ran past a danger signal and into bay platform No. 11 which at the time housed an empty DMU. This was the scene the following day with two of the DMU vehicles on the platform and a tangled mess of steel in the bay platform.* **David Ford**

Back Cover Bottom: *More than 120 passengers had a lucky escape on 6 March 1997, when the 15.35 Paddington to Penzance, formed of an HST set derailed on the approaches to Newton Abbot station in Devon. The derailment began with the inner end of the second passenger coach from the front which derailed and damaged the track allowing all following vehicles to go into derailment, the rear power car was derailed by only its inner bogie. The train was formed of Class 43 No. 43130, coaching stock set LA11 and power car No. 43170 on the rear. The train was derailed after a wheel bearing cut through the axle. Recovery was carried out by road cranes. The trains buffet car is seen lifted high from the crash scene.* **CJM**

Below: *At dawn on 17 November 2007 a serious side swipe collision occurred at the entrance of Leeds Neville Hill depot when two departing East Midlands Trains HST sets collided. The 04.09 Neville Hill to Sheffield empty stock was hit by the 04.17 Neville Hill to Sheffield empty stock movement. Power car No. 43059 of the second train collided violently with buffet car 40729 and FO 41113, with the two vehicles turning over. The buffet car was subsequently withdrawn. The derailment blocked the main line and recovery which was effected on 18 November required some of the overhead power equipment to be removed.* **Ron Cover**

Introduction

Welcome to *Modern Traction Rail Mishaps - A pictorial study of accidents, derailments and collisions*, a collection of fascinating and interesting pictures of UK railway accidents and operational problems.

Due to the nature of the rail transport industry using large and heavy machinery, when things go wrong or trains leave the track the results are often spectacular. This title, for which it has taken many years to collect the material bring together an unrivalled collection of illustrations, many of which have never been published before. Fresh research has revealed new information about several incidents.

In no way does this title try and glorify train accidents and mishaps, it portrays the end results to railway equipment after it has been involved in operational problems and many illustrations show the recovery operations underway, allowing a rare insight into the working and use of breakdown cranes.

Thankfully in the UK we see very very few major railway accidents, the evolved rules and regulations of our railway, together with a highly qualified and disciplined workforce ensures we have one of the safest rail passenger services in the world.

We hope you enjoy looking and reading this title and would be interested in seeing any pictures of railway mishaps that readers might have, as a further title *Rail Mishaps Vol 2* is on the cards.

Colin J. Marsden

Christopher G. Perkins

Contents

Early Modern Traction Mishaps

South Croydon

At 08.37 on the morning of 24 October 1947, during thick fog a rear end collision occurred 367 yards south of South Croydon Junction, when the eight car EMU formed 07.33 Haywards Heath to London Bridge was struck at around 40-45mph (64-72km/h)by the following 08.04 Tattenham Corner to London Bridge services formed on three 3-SUB units.

31 passengers and the motorman of the Tattenham Corner train were killed and more that 183 passengers were injured.

The cause of the accident, which was investigated by Lieut Colonel A. H. L. Mount, found that the signalman at Purley Oaks forgot the first train was stationary in his section towards South Croydon Junction, and then through the complete mis-use of the release key, cleared the signals for the following train to enter the section under a clear signal.

The impact was such that the leading coach of the Tattenham Corner train and the rear coach of the Haywards Heath service were almost totally destroyed and all deaths and serious injuries were within these vehicles.

Unlike today, the official reports comments on the quick return to use of the line, with all four tracks returning to normal just 24 hours later. ∎

Illustration: CJM Collection

Cricklewood

Depot mishaps are always a great embarrassment to staff and often costly to rectify in terms of line blockage and vehicle damage.

On Saturday 30 June 1962 green-liveried BRC&W Type 2, later Class 27 No. D5386 allocated to the London Midland Region, struck a suburban diesel-hydraulic Diesel Multiple Unit which was standing foul of points when departing from Cricklewood Carriage Sidings. This view was recorded just minutes after the impact with train crew and maintenance staff assessing the damage and working out a method of parting the trains without further damage. ∎

Illustration: Alex Swain

On 13 May 1966 the 23.00 class eight goods from Northwich to St. Helens, formed of 30 covered hoppers and one vanfit, all loaded with soda-ash and a brake van were hauled by an Ex-LMS Stanier 2-8-0 steam loco, having a total trailing weight of 1,195 tons.

Following a snatch, the train became divided between the second and third wagons on a falling gradient, as it continued onto a rising grade, the wagons lost momentum and eventually stopped, and then started running backwards. The guard quickly realised what had happened and applied his handbrake, but it was not enough to stop the run-away.

Between Norton Crossing and Acton Grange Junction they collided head-on at about 20mph (32km/h) with the 20.40 Euston to Stranraer hauled by EE Type 4 (later Class 40) No. D322 formed of 10 coaches. The cab of the loco was totally crushed and the driver and secondman were killed.

A fire broke out in the engine room but this was quickly extinguished.

It was established that the reason for the uncoupling was that some of the covered hoppers had 'through pipes' and needed longer buffers. The non-piped wagons were fitted with Instanter three-link couplings which were not long enough to couple to the piped wagons. Therefore the piped wagons had longer Continental screw couplings. The Continental coupling only fitted loosely over a normal threelink hook and during the snatch rode up and became detached. ∎
Illustration: R. J. Maxwell

In the days of un-fitted and part-fitted freight trains there was always a high risk of a run-away if the driver did not keep a firm hold of his train. Bearing in mind the only brake on the train was the straight air brake on the wheels of the locomotive or locomotives and a very lightly effective hand brake of the guards van.

After several brake efficiency problems on light weight diesel locomotives brake tenders were introduced by BR, these were literally a block of weight mounted on two four-wheel bogies fitted with vacuum brakes which increased the efficiency of the braking system. These could either be hauled or more frequently propelled by the locomotive.

One such run-away took place at Westhouses on 14 September 1968, when a loaded unfitted coal train was approaching Westhouses from the Teversal line and collided at speed with a rake of parked coal wagons.

The train was powered by a pair of English Electric Type 1s (later Class 20) and thankfully the footplate crew managed to jump out before impact.

The collision forced the leading locomotive sideways and onto its side, sustaining immense damage to the cab end and side bodywork, with the once leading cab being filled with coal, it is without doubt that the footplate crew would have been killed if they had not vacated the cab when they did. The view right shows the wreck before recovery work commenced with lesser damaged No. D8189 in the background. ∎
Illustration: Roger Varley

Bridgend

Eight month old Brush Type 4 (Class 47) No. D1671 *Thor* while powering the 04.00 Carmarthen to Bristol empty passenger stock working on 17 December 1965 ran into a major landslip at Bridgend which had been caused by heavy rain.

Upon impact, the train derailed and became foul of the adjacent 'down' running line. Almost immediately and before any alarm could be raised, the debris was struck by English Electric Type 3 (Class 37) No. D6983 heading the 02.30 Cardiff Tidal Docks to Swansea East Dock general merchandise freight train travelling in the opposite direction.

The impact caused a massive derailment of both trains and saw considerable damage to both locomotives. The drivers of both trains were sadly killed.

Although virtually new, the Brush Type 4 was deemed to be beyond economic repair as its frames were seriously damaged and it was officially condemned on 18 April 1966 following a period in store.

No. D1671 *Thor* was thus the first named loco of the class to be withdrawn. After parts were removed by BR engineers, the body was sold to R. S. Hayes scrap merchants at Bridgend and broken up, after a working life of less than nine months.

The *Thor* nameplates were later transferred to sister Type 4 No. D1677.

The English Electric Type 3, which was also less than one year old at the time of the accident fared no better, becoming the first member of the class to be withdrawn, and was also cut up at the same Bridgend scrapyard in 1966. ■

Illustrations: Main: CJM Collection
Inset: Norman E. Preedy

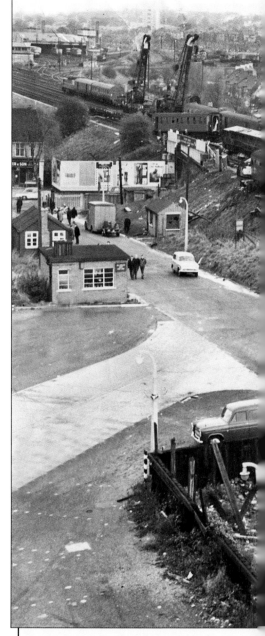

One of the most serious accidents to occur on British Railways Southern Region took place between Grove Park and Hither Green stations in south-east London at 21.16 on the evening of 5 November 1967.

The accident occurred, when the 19.43 Hastings to London Charing Cross express service formed of Class 6S No. 1007 and Class 6L 1017, derailed at approximately 70mph (113km/h), shortly before the train crossed the St Mildred's Road railway bridge.

The official inquiry held by the Ministry of Transport and conducted by Colonel D. McMullen, found the cause of derailment to be the leading pair of wheels of the third coach of the train hitting a wedge section of rail which had broken off from the running rail. This led the coach into derailment which veered in the direction of the down line, after around ¼ mile, the

derailed wheelset struck point and crossing work and led the coach ahead and all coupled in the rear into total derailment. The front coach split from the remainder and stopped still on the track just short of Hither Green station. Coaches 2-5 turned over onto their sides with vehicles 6-12 being derailed but upright.

Being a Sunday evening train from the coast, it was well filled and sadly 49 passengers died with a further 78 injured. At the time this made the Hither Green accident Britain's sixth worst rail disaster.

The accident enquiry looked at why the rail broke and found it occurred at a rail joint, with a fatigue crack passing through the first bolt hole which had progressively developed leading to a triangular piece of rail breaking off. The report concluded that it was probable that several previous trains had successfully negotiated the broken rail.

The track in general was heavily trafficked

by a dense outer suburban service of multiple unit trains, all of which has nose-suspended traction motors imposing high impact forces on the rail and any imperfection in the running surface of the rails.

The rail break was likely compounded by a poor track bed in the area, which led to a slight 'dipped rail joint' having high impact each time a wheel passed over it, thus increasing the speed in which the crack spread.

An interesting fact emerged from the inquiry, that the 'Hastings' DEMU stock was fitted with a special suspension system to limit sway of the bodies due to tight clearances in tunnels on the Tonbridge to Hastings line, and this caused very high wheel forces at track irregularities. This may be the reason why this particular train (rather than other trains which passed over the defect) derailed.

Speed was also a contributory factor, this had been raised from 75 mph (120km/h) to 90

Hither Green

mph (144km/h) in July 1967, and had not allowed for the level of increased maintenance required for higher speed running.

The Hither Green accident was attended by 33 ambulances and 28 fire appliances. Recovery of the trains was undertaken by rail mounted cranes from Hither Green, Stewarts Lane and Brighton and the line was fully returned to use by mid-day on 8 November 1967.

The view above shows the third to ninth vehicles of the train during recovery. The vast majority of vehicles were returned to service, with reformations allowing the displacement of buffet vehicle No. 60755 to be rebuilt as Southern Region General Managers Saloon No. DB975025. The vehicle is still in service today with Network Rail. ■

Illustration: CJM Collection

Hixon Crossing

LOCOMOTIVE

TRANSFORMER FROM LORRY

REAR OF TRANSPORTER

WRECKED SIGNAL BOX

TRACTOR

TRANSPORTER

LEVEL CROSSING

On 6 January 1968, a 120-ton electrical transformer was being moved from the English Electric works at Stafford to a storage depot on the disused airfield at Hixon, approximately three miles north of Colwich Junction on the West Coast Main Line.

A 32-wheeled, 148 ft (45 m) long cab and trailer unit weighing 162 tons owned by Wynns, and powered by a tractor unit at each end was used for the operation.

The transporter and a police escort left Stafford at approximately 09.30 on an agreed route which crossed the railway by way of Hixon crossing, however no Ministry of Transport map of the route made mention of the level crossing at Hixon.

At around 12.20 the transporter approached Hixon crossing at walking pace, it stopped for a moment and then proceeded at 2mph (3 km/h) while height adjustments were

carried out to clear the tracks as well as the 25kV overhead power lines. At 2mph it would take approximately one minute to pass over the crossing.

At 12.26, when the leading tractor had traversed the tracks and the main bulk of the transporter was astride them, the 11.30 Manchester Piccadilly to Euston activated the automatic half barrier crossing just 1000 yards (900m) away. Although the tractor drivers tried to drive the vehicle clear it was to no avail and the train hit the rear few feet of the transformer at approximately 75 mph (121 km/h). The impact sheared through the trailer and threw the transformer forward and to the left of the line.

The 11.30 Manchester Piccadilly to Euston was formed Class AL1 (Class 81) electric locomotive No. E3009 and 12 Mk1 passenger vehicles.

The locomotive and the first five coaches of the train were substantially demolished, and the following three coaches derailed. The tracks were destroyed for a length of 120 yards (110 m) and the overhead lines were brought down.

Eleven people, eight passengers and three railwaymen were killed, and 45 were injured.

After this accident the public outcry was such that a full Public Inquiry was called, this resulted in a 159 page official report.

The official cause of the accident was the failure of the haulage truck driver to stop as required and telephone the signalman before crossing the tracks.

Following this accident a huge change was made to the signage and instructions given to and by the police and haulage companies relating to the passage of large and slow vehicles over railway crossings. ∎

Illustration: CJM Collection

Gatwick Airport

Catch point derailments are frequently quite spectacular and cause quite serious damage to locomotives and rolling stock. Frequently such derailments, of which there have been many over the years, are difficult to effect a quick recovery due to land configuration.

An early catch point accident for a Birmingham RC&W Type 3 (later Class 33) occurred on 27 June 1964, when No. D6529 derailed near Gatwick Airport while powering a freight train. Recovery required the use of two Southern Region steam cranes, one from Brighton and the other from Stewarts Lane, which had to undertake a tandem lift, to raise the loco and then slew it back above repaired track.

Note the two spreader beams attached to the main hooks of the crane, onto which the lifting chains can be attached which are then attached to the locos fixed lifting points. ∎

Illustration: John Scrace

The short and steeply inclined 0.8mile (1.3km) branch linking Stourbridge Junction with Stourbridge Town has seen several accidents, all involving incidents at Stourbridge Town.

The first was on 15 June 1897 when a cattle and horse box train being propelled down the line suffered vacuum brake failure and collided with another train and the buffer stops. On 25 April 1905 a driver lost control of his locomotive while descending the branch with a rake of 32 wagons and crashed through the goods office.

A heavily loaded freight slipped away on the branch on 10 February 1948 even though the brakes were applied.

In the more modern era on 1 April 1977, single 'Bubble' car No. M55012 suffered brake failure while descending the branch and crashed through the buffer stops, ending up partly hanging over the street below (illustrated above).

A more unusual accident occurred on 21 January 1989 when trespassers on the line distracted the driver of a single car DMU

Stourbridge Town

causing him to misjudge his braking distance, with the train hitting the buffer stops and crashing through a wall. On 1 March 1990 a brake failure is reported to have caused another single car to overshoot the stopping point and collide with the wall at the end of the line. ■

Illustration: Joma Enterprises

Itchingfield Jn

Another serious accident to befall a BRC&W Type 3 (Class 33) 'Crompton' was on 5 March 1964, when No. D6502 was involved in a serious collision at Itchingfield Junction (south of Christ's Hospital) where the Horsham-Arundel and Horsham-Shoreham lines parted.

No. D6502 powering a freight train, over-ran a red signal and crashed into the back of a ballast train. The loco ended up on its side with its entire underframe and bogies stripped off with extensive body damage. Repairs were not possible and the loco was broken up on site by BR engineers. The loco was officially withdrawn in May 1964. ■

Illustration: John Scrace

Modern Traction Rail Mishaps - A pictorial study

Run through accidents involving the overshooting of sidings and running through catch points was always a possibility with part brake or unfitted freight trains. Even with the most experienced drivers one seconds lapse of concentration or a release of the straight air brake (regenerative brake in the case of the 'Tommy' dc electrics), could see a signal missed and the train stop in the wrong, often disastrous place.

Two such accidents occurred at Torside, mid way across the Pennines between Manchester

and Sheffield in February 1956 and March 1957. In both cases trains overshot the loop track and ran through the sand drag and into railway buildings.

The accident in March 1957 involved Class EM1 (later Class 76) Bo-Bo 1,500V dc electric No. E26040, which at the time was still painted in BR main line black livery.

The loco, powering a mineral train went past the signal in the loop at danger, went through the sand drag, demolished the buffer stops past through a section of the footbridge and collided

Torside

with a lineside railway building, demolishing part of the fencing by the road crossing. The locomotive was derailed all wheels and sustained serious underframe damage and some front and side damage, the following six wagons were derailed all wheels. Recovery of the loco was difficult, with it eventually craned onto the adjacent main line. ∎

Illustrations: CJM Collection

Cotton Hill Shrewsbury

Brush Type 4 (later Class 47) No. D1734 had charge of a class five freight train from Saltney Yard near Chester to Pontypool Road on the morning of 11 January 1965.

The train was formed of 46 wagons and a guards brake van, of which 245 tons were braked and 530 tons were un-braked making a total train weight of 775 tons.

On the approach to Shrewsbury from the Wrexham direction there is a long downhill stretch ending in a 1:100 on the approach to the station known as Hencote Incline.

At the top of this incline was a stop board which required all class five freights to stop before proceeding down the gradient. At about 05.50, No. D1734 passed the stop board without stopping, the train was then signalled into the goods loop at Cotton Hill North Signalbox but because it had not been brought to a stand at the top of the incline, it was now travelling too fast to enable it to stop at the red signal at the bottom of the downgrade.

It lurched over the points into the loop but remained on the rails, the driver by this time making a full brake application but this made no impression on the trains speed. At the end of the goods loop the locomotive ran through the catchpoints protecting the mainline and continued off the rails for some 70 yards (64m) when it then demolished Cotton Hill South signalbox sadly killing the signalman on duty at the time, coming to rest beyond the box.

The first 11 wagons of the train followed the locomotive into derailment but as the locomotive went through the signalbox it damaged the signalling frame which opened up a point in the loop to a siding which caused a further 24 wagons to enter this siding and derail some colliding with a further Brush Type 4 (Class 47) No. D1684.

When the locomotive was examined by railway and Ministry engineers after the accident, the brakes were found to be working normally but the Automatic Warning System (AWS) was found to be isolated.

This accident was caused by the driver failing to stop in accordance with the rule book at the top of the incline and then proceeding.

No. D1734 was new to Bristol Bath Road in May 1964, but it was so badly damaged it was withdrawn and cut up after a working life of just eight months. ∎

Illustration: Top: Colour-rail.com
Above left and Above right: CJM Collection

Chester

BR Type 2, later Class 24 No. 5028 had charge of 38 wagons forming the 19.30 Ellesmere Port to Mold Junction via Helsby where it reversed on the evening of 9 May 1972. The first five vehicles of the train were tank wagons containing petrol, gas oil and kerosene.

Approaching Chester, on a falling gradient of 1:100 at about 20.50, the driver applied the brakes but found he had insufficient brake power to stop his train. It ran past a danger signal and into bay platform 11 which at the time housed an empty DMU.

Realising that he was still unable to stop his train the driver jumped clear onto the platform whilst the train was travelling at about 20mph (32km/h), sustaining some injuries. The Class 24 impacted the DMU with such force that it completely destroyed the rear coach and pushed the front coach onto the platform ripping off its bogies in the process and crashing into the station building, partly demolishing the refreshment room wall.

Nobody was injured on the platform, but the refreshment room staff had to take shelter from falling brickwork. Very quickly a massive fire broke out in the tank wagons and passengers from an adjacent train had to be evacuated as it also caught fire. The fire was severe, and was not extinguished until 00.20 the next day.

All the vehicles involved in the incident were written off and scrapped, mainly on site.

The enquiry found that the train had departed from Ellesmere Port as an unfitted freight but with eight vacuum braked wagons at the rear, which would then be at the front on reversal at Helsby giving the required extra braking power for the 1:100 descent into Chester. But on running round at Helsby the guard forgot to connect up the vacuum pipe and the driver failed to carry out the statutory brake test, rendering the train crew responsible for the accident. ∎

Illustrations: All David Ford

The 13.00 Birmingham Snow Hill to Paddington was normally operated by a Blue Pullman diesel set by 1963, but on 20 August 1963 the set was out of service and the train was operated by Class 52 No. D1040 *Western Queen* and nine Pullman coaches.

The signalman at Bentley Heath Crossing accepted the train, which was travelling on the up main line into his section, and he also received train accepted from the Knowle & Dorridge signalbox. He then cleared all his signals.

However, the signalman at Knowle & Dorridge forgot he had accepted the train

Knowle

and did not clear his signals. He then allowed a shunting move consisting of an Ex-GWR Pannier tank propelling a 20 ton brake van, an empty carflat, and a carflat loaded with Land Rovers onto the up main line.

The Pullman, travelling at around 80mph (132km/h) and on seeing that the distant signal for Knowle & Dorridge was at danger, the driver made an emergency brake application, but the distance between the distant signal and home signal was only 902 yards (824.7m), and was insufficient distance for the train to stop.

The signalman realised his mistake and managed to stop the shunt move but there was not enough time for it to reverse out of the way. The 'Western' struck the loaded carflat at approximately 20mph (32km/h), the whole of the train stayed on the rails but the cab was totally destroyed. The four-crew members from the freight managed to jump clear and were uninjured but sadly the three crew in the cab of the 'Western' were killed. The driver was Ernest Morris who had featured in the British Transport Film *Lets Go To Birmingham*. ■
Illustration: Paul Riley

Drumlanrigg

Running into earth slips has always been a major problem on the railway, as little lineside equipment can detect such events, and often slips can happen in far away places from staffed areas.

On the night of 13/14 August 1966, English Electric Type 4 (later Class 40) No. D311 ran into a landslide at Ardoch in the Drumlanrigg Gorge between Dumfries and Sanquhar while powering train 1M13, the 22.25 Glasgow Central to London Euston sleeping car express.

The Type 4 and several passenger vehicles were totally derailed with the loco landing up at nearly 45deg towards its side.

Recovery was carried out by two 75 ton heavy recovery cranes, one facing either direction which between them performed a tandem lift of the 100 ton plus loco body. No. D311 was repaired after this accident at BREL Crewe Works and returned to main line traffic in less than one year.

No. D311 was also involved in two further incidents before being withdrawn, the most serious being on 26 October 1975 when it collided at around 25mph (40.2km/h) with the rear of a train which it was required to assist between Montrose and Arbroath. Both the illustrations on the opposite page show the recovery operation at Drumlanrigg Gorge. ■
Illustrations: Derek Cross

Stoke-on-Trent

Railwaymen and passers by inspect the damage at Stoke-on-Trent on 22 October 1985, after Class 25s Nos. 25058 and 25213 powering a sand train from Longport to Oakamoor derailed near Stoke signal box and collided with the buffer stops before demolishing a wall and coming to rest over hanging the road below.

Thankfully nobody was injured on the street below considering the amount of brickwork and steel which fell.

The incident was blamed on human error on the part of the driver for failing to control his train. ■
Illustration: B. G. Hughes

The Devastation of Train Fires

Lochside

In April 1977. a Class 126 Inter-City DMU was travelling between Glasgow and Ayr. One of the engines under car No. 51028 had not reversed and was thus being driven backwards at full throttle. This eventually caused a major fire, which burned out the carriage, fortunately without casualties. No. 51028 is seen the day after standing in the loop at Lochside awaiting dismantling (it was deformed out of gauge). It is surprising how such heat can cause even a strong Mk 1 carriage underframe to sag!

In the view left, the interior of No. 51028 shows the total destruction by fire of all fabrics, timbers and plastics.

The failure to reverse the engine suggests that the driver had not diligently checked that all the final drive detection lamps had gone out and re-lit when he reversed the train at Glasgow Central. ■

Illustrations: Colin Boocock

Brighton

A serious depot fire at Brighton Lovers Walk occurred in autumn 1975, when the Driving Motor Brake Second 61036 caught fire, which spread to the adjacent TC vehicle No. 70038. Thankfully being 'on shed' no injuries were sustained. The DMBS vehicle was broken up on site, while the lesser damaged TC vehicle was later transferred to East Wimbledon depot to donate parts before moving to BREL Eastleigh Works. The vehicle is seen at East Wimbledon in March 1976. ■
Illustration: CJM

This very sad sight was recorded at Scotland's Eastfield depot on 7 August 1982, when the remains of Class 27/0 No. 27043 were seen at the depot after a serious cab fire at the

Eastfield

No. 2 end which had totally destroyed the cab, melted the cab roof and spread to the electrical equipment in the engine room.

The loco was subsequently broken up as uneconomic to repair. ■

Illustration: Derek Porter

In recent years a growing trend of depot vandalism has sadly seen a number of fires, resulting in many vehicles being destroyed.

One such incident took place at Old Oak Common in west London during mid-2006 resulting in a number of charter Mk1 and Mk2 vehicles being

Old Oak Common

destroyed. Pullman-liveried Mk2 TSO No. 5389 awaits disposal on 30 December 2006. ■

Illustration: Tony Christie

Kensal Green

It is always especially sad to recount accidents close to Christmas, however on Christmas Eve 1977, a very serious near head-on collision occurred between Union Jack-liveried Class 47 No. 47163, painted in support of the Queens 1977 Silver Jubilee and Class 83 electric No. 83004 near Kensal Green Tunnel in north west London.

The Class 83 was piloting Class 82 No. 82001 and approaching Willesden depot, when they were struck head-on and at speed by train 4E68, the 04.50 Willesden Freightliner Terminal to Tilbury container train powered by the Class 47. The impact was so severe the Class 83 broke its back and the two leading cabs of both the Class 47 and 83 became completely entangled.

A major fire soon broke out engulfing the cabs of both locos, which sadly claimed the life of the driver on the Class 47.

Recovery of the locomotives took place over the Christmas period, with all three taken to the nearby Willesden depot. The overhead electrics were withdrawn from service as uneconomic to repair, while the Class 47 was taken to BREL Crewe and fully repaired returning to service almost two years later. ■

Illustrations: CJM Collection

Modern Traction Rail Mishaps - A pictorial study

Eccles

A very serious rear end collision occurred on 4 December 1984 at Eccles, Greater Manchester, when an express passenger train collided at speed with the rear of a freight train of oil tankers. The driver of the passenger train and two passengers were killed, and 68 people were injured.

The passenger train involved was the 10.05 Liverpool Lime Street to Scarborough, formed of Class 45 'Peak' No. 45147, seven passenger coaches and a parcels van. The freight train was the 09.00 service from Stanlow Oil Refinery at Ellesmere Port to Leeds, formed of Class 47 No. 47310 and 15 bogie tank wagons containing fuel oil.

The freight had just passed Eccles station and was starting to accelerate away when the passenger train, having passed both the Eccles distant signal at caution and the home signal at danger, collided at nearly 50mph (80km/h) with its rear end.

The force of the impact threw the rear tank wagon to the side, but the next two were tossed into the air, with one falling back onto the passenger train loco and first coach.

The wagons were very badly damaged and escaping fuel ignited, setting fire to No. 45147 and the leading two coaches. Fortunately, the leading coach was empty of passengers or the death toll would probably have been higher.

Rescue efforts were assisted as the location was adjacent to the M602 motorway, enabling easy access for emergency services.

The inquiry into the accident found that the driver of the passenger train had missed the Eccles signals and was responsible for the accident. The signals were not fitted with AWS. ∎

Illustrations: Top: Alan Sherratt,
Above & Below: John Tuffs

Ealing
19 December 1973

Locomotive:	D1007 *Western Talisman*
Stock:	Mk1
Train:	17.18 Paddington-Oxford
Accident Type:	Derailment
Passengers on train:	650
Fatalities:	10
Injuries:	94

Just six days before Christmas 1973 a catastrophic accident befell the 17.18 Paddington to Oxford commuter train as it passed below Longfield Road bridge between Ealing and West Ealing when travelling at around 70mph (113km/h).

The train was powered by 'Western' Class 52 No. D1007 *Western Talisman*, which during the course of the day had received maintenance at Old Oak Common depot, little known to the footplate crew, during this work, the battery boxes had been opened but had not been locked closed. As the train headed out of London, gaining speed, one of the bottom hinged batterybox doors on the drivers side in the direction of travel opened, the door fell open at a 45 deg angle until it struck the platform edge at Ealing Broadway. This impact ripped off the door brackets with the door flap dropping down vertically.

Soon after passing through Ealing Broadway station, the batterybox door struck a point motor box controlling movement from the down main line to the down local line via the up main track. The impact with the point motor opened the point switch and the rear wheels of the loco and entire train went into derailment.

The loco flipped over onto its side, as did the second coach of the train, with coaches 2-6 ending up in a concertina pattern diagonal to the direction of travel.

The train quickly came to a stand and thankfully was not hit by any other service. However, 10 passengers on the train were killed and over 90 injured.

The accident was investigated by the railway inspectorate and the cause identified as the failure to secure the battery box door. In addition to the un-securing of the battery box door, a safety 'pear-drop' clip which should have automatically dropped to prevent opening had been secured in an open position. ●

Above: *Taken in the early hours of 20 December 1973 after the dead and injured had been removed from the twisted wreckage. The Old Oak Common-based steam recovery crane starts removing debris from the slow line tracks before tackling the recovery of the passenger stock and locomotive. Back in 1973 the recovery was carried out by all rail-mounted recovery cranes, unlike the present day when road mounted high-capacity cranes are used in most rail accidents. The largely undamaged No. D1007* Western Talisman *lays in the foreground.* **CJM**

Left: *The position where the battery box door from No. D1007* Western Talisman *should have been attached. After the door opened soon after departure from London, it fell downwards, hitting lineside furniture before hitting and moving a set of facing points at Longfield Road, Ealing.* **CJM**

Right: *Soon after investigators arrived at the scene of the West Ealing accident, it was quickly found that something had struck the point motor box controlling a pair of facing points at Longfield Road, debris in the area suggested it was part of the locomotive and within hours it was identified as the locos battery box door being open and striking the point machine and thus causing the point blades to open from the correct position were the prime cause of the accident. This view shows the point machine as it was found by investigators, with its cast iron and steel shell destroyed by the heavy impact.* **CJM**

Up relief line

To West Ealing and Reading

To Ealing and Paddington

Down relief line

Up main line

D1007

W26068

W26097

W15777

W16322

W13353

W21147

W26068

W25097

W26164

W26106

W26133

Down main line

Vehicles on side
(all other vehicles remained upright)

Position where battery
box door was found

Position of point motor
struck by battery box door

Above: *Map showing the position in which vehicles and the locomotive landed after the impact and derailment. The most serious deformation of the train occurred at the front, with the train travelling at speed over the defective points work, dragging the locomotive onto its side. The four vehicles at the rear of the train escaped without major damage and were returned to traffic.* **CJM**

Left & Right: *Four views showing the recovery work underway on the day following the derailment. Removal of the wreckage took some four days to complete with the main line tracks closed to passenger services for about a week. Recovery of the passenger vehicles and locomotive was a complex operation with restrictive access as the line was in a slight cutting with difficult road access. Three heavy lift steam and diesel recovery cranes were involved with removal of wreckage with all items taken by rail to Old Oak Common yard. Some of the more badly damaged vehicles were broken up on site, but as much as possible was recovered to take part in the investigation process.* **CJM**

Wagons, Wagons Everywhere

Chinley

Class 47/0 No. 47089 *Amazon* which was allocated to Bristol Bath Road depot at the time had charge of train 7A22, the 14.32 Peak Forest to Bletchley loaded stone train on 20 February 1987.

It was reported that the train was overloaded, and also that it was likely the last four wagon brakes had been isolated.

The train ran away down the 1:90 gradient approaching Chinley North Junction and was derailed on catchpoints protecting the junction.

At the same time as the derailment, Class 31/4 No. 31440 which was hauling train 1M34, the 16.22 Sheffield to Liverpool Lime Street was approaching and was unable to stop in time, crashing into the derailed wagons.

Recovery was a complex operation, requiring the use of two 75 ton lift capacity rail-mounted cranes, which first had to clear a mess of tangled wagons before recovery of the locomotives could be

undertaken. The Class 47 landed up on its side and had to be righted before it could be recovered from the site by rail.

No. 47089 was then stored at Buxton Depot and was eventually taken to BREL Crewe Works where it was stripped of usable parts before being taken to Coopers Metals of Sheffield for disposal in 1989.

No. 31440 was dumped in sidings at Hope for some time and was also withdrawn it was subsequently stripped of parts at BREL Doncaster before being cut up by Vic Berry of Leicester. ■

Illustrations: Above & Left: Colin Boocock, Below: CJM

Pandy

On the morning of 18 August 1965, Brush Type 4 (Class 47) No. D1584, which was just 15 months old, was heading a coal and steel train when at Pandy, five miles north of Abergavenny, it was diverted into a siding.

Unable to stop, it crashed through the buffer stops and became embedded into the embankment, with the train piling up behind it and destroying the rear cab.

The crew jumped from the loco before impact, and the driver suffered leg injuries. Both main lines on the Newport to Shrewsbury route were blocked for 12 hours. No. D1584 ended its career as No. 47775 and was cut up at Crewe in 2006. ∎

Illustration: D. H. Cape

Hungerford

A defective wheelset on an ARC JHA bogie hopper wagon led to a serious derailment at Hungerford Loop of the 05.45 Whatley to Southall aggregate train on 5 September 1994.

The train was formed of 43 wagons and eight in the middle of the formation derailed. Recovery of the train was carried out by staff and the heavy lift recovery crane from Old Oak Common.

After the derailment, the entire fleet of JHA wagons were taken out of service until repairs could be undertaken. ∎

Illustrations: Bob Pratley

Cogload Junction

On the morning of 18 August 1986, a southbound Cement service formed of 18 four-wheeled PCA tank wagons, powered by Class 47 No. 47144 derailed just South of Cogload Junction, Taunton causing a major accident. The then four track mainline was closed while the huge clear up operation took place, with single lines later reopened to traffic once wagons had been cleared from the running lines and track repaired.

The train, which originated from the Blue Circle Industries plant at Westbury and operated west by way of Castle Cary, derailed due to the collapse of an overheated wheelset. This was caused by the train travelling all the way from Westbury with a handbrake applied, this had caused a double flange on the wheel, which derailed on striking pointwork at Cogload Junction. The hand brake was left applied due to an improperly managed train preparation procedure at Westbury.

Recovery of the train was quite complex and required all four tracks to be blocked. The Bristol based recovery team arrived with their tool vans but without a crane as this was under repair at the time. The crane based at Plymouth Laira was deemed as too light, so cranes were eventually supplied by Cardiff Canton and Eastleigh.

Repairs were advanced enough by 17.00 on 20 August to allow single line working to be set up. Two track working was resumed the following day.

The view above and left show the Eastleigh-based 75 tonne diesel-hydraulic crane powered by Class 37 No. 37203 dealing with recovery operations on 19 August 1986. ∎
Illustrations: Paul Clarke

Cupar

A derailment which had tremendous effects on the local area took place at Cupar in Scotland on the main Edinburgh to Dundee route on 2 June 1988.

A cement train formed of four-wheeled PCA 'Presflow' wagons derailed and ripped up more than a 1000m of track and in the process one of the wagons collided with a support of the B940 road bridge which crossed above the line. The impact ripped the bridge down closing the Cupar to Perth road.

The wagons on the train were seriously damaged and many were broken up on site.

In the view above, recorded on 4 June 1988 the remains of four wagons can be seen with the destroyed road bridge above.

Trains were diverted via Perth for three days after the accident, with recovery and rebuilding of the bridge taking months to complete. ■

Illustration: Alan Mitchell

Derby

Services through Derby were seriously disrupted on 12 July 1978 after a collision occurred between an empty Merry-Go-Round coal train and an empty passenger train pulling off Derby Etches Park depot. A number of the HAA coal hoppers derailed and several overturned. The area around London Road Junction was blocked for more than 24 hours while recovery was undertaken. ■

Illustration: John Tuffs

North Staffs Jnc

A northbound mineral train passing over North Staffs Junction between Burton-on-Trent and Derby where the Crewe line joins the Birmingham to Derby route derailed several wagons on 18 August 1977. From the illustration it appears the wagons derailed when passing over the point work of the Crewe line. This is the view looking south from the accident scene soon after the incident. ■

Illustration: John Tuffs

Maidstone East

Train 6M57, the 01.20 Dover Town to Willesden Brent Sidings on 6 September 1993 was formed of Class 47/0 No. 47288 and 15 air-braked ferry wagons making a trailing load of 907 tonnes.

Maidstone East Station is on a sharp curve with a speed restriction through the station of 25mph (40km/h). At 02.12 the train became derailed as it passed through the station. The locomotive and first wagon turned onto their right sides. The second and third wagons entered the station sideways demolishing the Dover end of the structure on the down platform, shearing all except one of the cast-iron canopy columns and badly damaging other parts of the building.

Eight wagons remained upright and on the track.

Research at the scene calculated the derailment speed as between 60 and 74mph (96-119km/h) and the speed of the locomotive when it overturned being 70mph (113km/h).

The driver was taken to Maidstone Hospital but had only suffered bruising to the ribs. He was discharged from the hospital 2½ hours after the accident when he was then, as a matter of routine, bretherlised.

At the lowest reading obtained he was found to be nearly four times over the limit specified in the Transport and Works Act 1992.

Recovery was a complex operation and used both rail and road cranes over a period of five days. ∎

Illustrations: John Chalcraft

Modern Traction Rail Mishaps - A pictorial study

Pont's Mill

On 9 March 2005 the Goonbarrow to Fowey Docks china clay train in Cornwall, formed of CDA wagons derailed on Prideaux Viaduct near Pont's Mill, St. Blazey. The 18th wagon of the train had derailed approximately two thirds of the way across the viaduct. A further 14 wagons then derailed with only the last two remaining on the track.

The derailed wagons caused extensive damage to the track beyond the viaduct with several wagons being in danger of toppling over into the adjacent river.

The accident was due to gauge widening on the longitudinal timbers of the viaduct. This was caused by displaced packings, incorrect setting of transom bolts and decay in the left hand timber. ■

Illustration: Nathan Stockman

As DB Schenker's 6C99, the 05.50 service from Newport Alexandra Dock Junction was setting back into the yard at it's destination of St. Blazey, Cornwall on 9 June 2010, the leading wagon, Imerys JIA 'Polybulk' No. 33 70 0894 017-9 split the points and ended up at right angles to the route.

This closed the Par-Newquay branch completely and several freight workings were also cancelled. The wagon was eventually re-railed with the assistance of the Bescot

St. Blazey

breakdown train, which was brought to the scene by Class 66 No. 66141. ■

Illustration: Nathan Stockman

Foxhall Junction

The new year of 1966 did not start well for British Rail Western Region, when Brush Type 4 (later Class 47) No. D1775 crashed through buffer stops at Foxhall Junction, Didcot, while powering an 'up' freight on 1 January 1966. The loco landed up laying on its side with the train crushing into the rear cab leaving a heap of destroyed wagons. The loco was eventually recovered and repaired at Crewe Works. This loco later became No. 47180 under the 1973 TOPS system and was renumbered to 47584 after fitting electric train heat. This view shows the loco on its side surrounded by a heap of wagons. ■
Illustration: CJM Collection

Par

On 20 June 1989, the Cornish main line was in chaos, after a westbound china clay train formed of modern ECC air braked four-wheeled wagons derailed as it headed towards the main line at Par after departure from St Blazey Yard, eight wagons derailed with at least one turning over depositing china clay powder all over the track.

Recovery was effected by the team from Plymouth Laira with the depots crane and tool vans attending. A Class 47 can be seen with the three tool vans, while a Class 37 assists with the crane. ■
Illustration: C. D. Jones

Sleeper Trains in Distress

Prestonpans

On the evening of 22 May 1980, a vandal wedged a near 6ft (2m) length of cut rail weighing around 2cwt between the rails of the up main Edinburgh to London King's

Cross line at Prestonpans.

The short rail had been left on site during previous civil engineering work. When the Class 47 heading the night sleeping car train from Aberdeen to London hit the rail it bounced along under the train for some distance, before forcing the track to spread

under the third vehicle, this causing the train to derail totally rearward of the third coach.

Fortunately no-one was significantly injured, and there was no train on the opposite track at the time.

The rail breakdown crane could not easily reach most vehicles in the train so large road cranes were hired to help clear the site.

With modern buck-eye couplings the Mk1 formed train stayed upright and mostly in line with one vehicle landing up at a 45deg angle.

A police investigation found that the rail had been placed on the track in an attempt to derail the train by a 17 year old youth, who was said to have had women problems,who was later apprehended and sent to borstal. ∎

Illustrations: Colin Boocock

Morpeth

At 01.31 on 7 May 1969 train 1S60, the 19.40 London King's Cross to Aberdeen sleeper, *The Night Aberdonian*, hauled by Class 55 'Deltic' No. D9011 *The Royal Northumberland Fusiliers* and formed of 11 Mk1 coaches of which four were sleeping cars, derailed on the curve prior to Morpeth station.

The speed restriction on the Morpeth curve is just 40mph (64km/h)but on this night the train entered the curve at between 80 and 84mph (129-135km/h).

The train's driver admitted that he had become distracted because shortly before leaving Newcastle he had been handed a notice about being four minutes late on a previous trip. He had been trying to work out in his mind where he had lost these minutes and it was only when the secondman realised that they were travelling too fast for the curve that a brake application was made, but it was too late to reduce the speed of the train.

Behind the locomotive, Mk1 brake No. M81300 derailed on the curve and as it overturned it brought the rest of the train into derailment behind it. The locomotive continued on and came to a stand in Morpeth station 508 yards past the point of derailment.

It had dragged the brake van with it, which by now was just the frame with no body or bogies. Five passengers and a Travelling Ticket Inspector were killed, 121 passengers were injured. ∎

Illustrations: John M. Boyes

Modern Traction Rail Mishaps - A pictorial study

Nuneaton

During June 1975 there was a major track-remodelling scheme carried out at Nuneaton and a 20mph (32km/h) speed restriction was imposed through the station over a temporary section of track, which had a severe curve in it.

The restriction had been in place since the weekend of 24/25 May 1975. One mile before the restriction there was an advanced warning board giving notice of the restriction and at night the speed numerals on the board would be illuminated by two gas lamps.

On 6 June 1975 the Glasgow sleeper train had left Euston on time at 23.30 the previous evening, hauled by Class 86/2 No. 86242 and formed of 12 sleeping cars, one buffet car and two passenger brake vans.

The Class 86 failed at Kings Langley and another Class 86 No. 86006 was sent from Willesden to assist. This was attached to the front of the train on top of the dead loco, saving time in detaching the failed locomotive. The train continued its journey some 75 minutes late.

On the night of the accident, several trains had passed the advanced speed restriction board for the Nuneaton remodelling work and had noted that the warning lamps were not illuminated, but none of the drivers had reported the situation. But all had observed the temporary speed restriction. The Glasgow sleeper passed the site of the advanced warning board at approximately 80mph (129km/h), the driver assumed that as he

did not see the unlit marker board, that the speed restriction had been lifted.

It was not until he saw the correctly lit speed commencement board at the start of the restriction that he realised that it was still in force. He made an emergency brake application but it was far too late and the train entered the temporary track section at over 70mph (113km/h) and became derailed. It was later estimated that the maximum speed the temporary track could be negotiated without derailment was 45mph.

In the derailment the locomotives became detached from each other, with Class 86/2 No. 86242 mounting the northbound platform and causing extensive damage to the station. Every coach except the last one was derailed, the first two remained upright but the following four turned onto their sides and were very badly crushed. All the fatalities and the majority of the injuries were from these four coaches.

Two passengers and two sleeping car attendants died at the scene and a further two passengers died later in hospital, 38 passengers were injured 10 of which were seriously injured. The injury toll could have been much higher had it not been for the train being fairly lightly loaded with less than 100 passengers on board.

Three overhead electrification gantries along with a quarter of a mile of track were totally destroyed along with damage to a road over bridge support piers, plus numerous items of lineside equipment including point machines and electrical control boxes. Also Class 25 No. 25286, which was heading a freight train in the

opposite direction, received some damage when one of the overhead gantries fell onto it.

Due to the large amount of damage to the infrastructure the down and up slow lines were not reopened to electric traction until 22.00 on 10 June 1975, and the fast lines remained blocked until 14.30hrs on 12 June 1975.

During this period main line services were diverted via Birmingham while road transport was used for local services.

Major C. F. Rose who conducted the inquiry into the accident found that it was due to 1) The gas equipment that powered the warning lights on the advance warning board was not being used properly which allowed the lights to go out. 2) A number of drivers on preceding trains who had seen that the lights were out, failed to report this fact, even though they were required to do so in accordance with the Rule Book. 3) Although the driver claimed otherwise, Major Rose thought it likely that the driver of the Glasgow sleeper train in his haste to regain lost time following the earlier failure, forgot about the speed restriction without the reminder of the advanced warning board.

The driver was later charged with six cases of manslaughter but was found not guilty at Birmingham Crown Court in 1976.

Major Rose felt that if an AWS magnet had been installed at the site of the advanced warning board, even if the lights had been out, the driver would have received an audible warning of the speed restriction ahead and if not acknowledged would have activated the brakes. ■

Illustration: CJM Collection

Paddington

Train 1A07, the 21.35 Penzance to Paddington sleeper service departed on 22 November 1983 formed of Class 50 No. 50041 *Bulwark* and after the Plymouth stop was formed of 14 coaches, four of which were Mk3 sleeping coaches with total train weight of 606 tons.

The train departed from Reading the following morning right time and ran normally until about two miles from Paddington where, instead of slowing to observe the 60mph (96km/h) speed restriction, it continued at speed. It was still travelling at over 65mph (105km/h) when it entered a crossover half a mile outside Paddington station over which the maximum permitted speed was 25mph (40km/h).

The excessive speed caused the locomotive to derail and after running off the tracks for some distance it separated from its train and overturned onto its left side, coming to rest straddling the rails at the side of platform eight under Bishop's Bridge having travelled over 1,300 ft (400m) completely derailed.

The leading 12 coaches also became completely derailed, some turning on their sides or ending up leaning over at various angles.

The 13th coach had one axle derailed and the 14th remained totally on the rails.

The driver claimed that he had made a brake application in the normal place and although the brake pipe gauges showed normal indications the train did not slow down. He then made a full emergency brake application followed by applying the locomotive straight air brake none of which slowed the train.

The inquiry found that although it had been a very cold night with freezing fog and a temperature of minus 5 centigrade at Swindon, there was no evidence of the brakes failing due to freezing.

It was therefore concluded that the driver probably lost concentration or possibly dozed off to light sleep on the approach to Paddington, and when he did realise where he was, the brake applications he made were far too late to slow the train down before arriving at the point of derailment.

Amazingly only three passengers were taken to hospital with minor injuries, and none were detained.

Recovery of the train and loco were a very complex affair, with three rail borne recovery cranes involved. The lines into Paddington were not fully re-opened for more than a week.

Class 50 No. 50041 *Bulwark* was dragged out from below the bridge, uprighted and taken to Old Oak Common. It was subsequently taken to BREL Doncaster and rebuilt for main line use. ∎

Illustrations: Colour: Jeremy De-Souza
Monochrome: Barry Edwards

Walton-on-Naze

A buffer stop collision took plate at Walton-on-Naze station on 12 August 1987, when Class 313 dual-voltage EMU No. 313063 forming the 13.05 Thorpe-le-Soken to Walton-on-Naze collided with the buffer stops at between 10-15mph (16-24km/h).

Seven people on the train needed hospital treatment, but were not seriously injured.

The incident was investigated by the Health & Safety Executive with Major C. B. Holden acting as chair.

The report found that while a brake defect did exist on the train, the overall cause of the accident was the failure of the driver to apply his brake valve early enough, and even after realising that no appreciable speed retardation was being made, failed to make use of the emergency position of the brake, which if used earlier would have avoided a collision.

The impact with the buffer stops, saw the leading coach of the train No. 62655 part from its lead bogie and collide with the station building, seriously damaging the gentlemen's toilet block, station roof and fencing.

The Class 313 was fully repaired and returned to traffic. This accident resulted in major changes in driver training in respect to brake controller use. ■

Illustrations: Colin Brooks

Slough

One of the major problems with modern multiple unit stock is the use of off-wheelface braking, which in slippery greasy rail conditions can lead to problems. This is compounded by trains being fitted with 'blow-down' equipment which reduces the brake pressure on any given wheelset if wheels are thought by onboard electronics to have wheel slip or slide.

When the Class 165 and 166 Turbo units were introduced by Network SouthEast a number of drivers complained about poor braking efficiency in slippery autumn rail conditions and a number of minor station run-bys were reported.

On the evening of 2 November 1993 things came to a head, when Reading-based Turbo No. 165102, forming the 19.41 all stations service from Paddington to Slough slipped on the approach to the bay platform at Slough and collided heavily with the buffer stops. The force of the impact sheered off the leading bogie, which then acted as a 'launch pad' for the coach and

pushed it deep into the station buildings ending up totally wedged in the station building. The leading end of the middle coach also climbed into the station building.

Thankfully being a lightly loaded evening departure at the end of its journey few passengers were on the train and only the driver and one member of station staff were slightly injured.

Recovery of the train was very difficult, the London end driving car was removed by rail, while much of the station iron work associated with the canopy had to be removed to recover the leading and middle vehicles, these were taken away by road to Derby for investigation and repair.

The cause of the accident was found to be poor adhesion in slippery rail conditions, which led to revised handling techniques being issued to drivers. In the long term, this accident and other incidents paved the way to the installation of sanders to improve wheel-rail adhesion in poor rail head conditions. ∎

Illustration: CJM Collection

Redditch

Low adhesion and the use of modern off-wheel braking was also the cause of the first Class 323 accident on 3 October 1994, when set No. 323205 collided with the buffer stops at Redditch while forming the 17.52 Lichfield to Redditch service.

The train after making a perfectly good run over the Birmingham Cross-City route attempted to reduce speed for its final stop and slid into the platform, also experiencing brake blow down and the on-board equipment had detected wheel slip/slide. The train impacted the buffer stops at around 5mph (8km/h) and pushed them forward a complete coach length before the train came to a stand. The leading vehicle No. 65005 sustained some front end and underside damage. No passengers were injured and the driver was just shaken and able to walk from the cab.

Recovery was undertaken by the road/rail BRUFF unit from Tyseley and used jacks to rerail the vehicle. Two Class 31s Nos. 31106/237 were also sent down the branch to assist in hauling the set back onto the track. The set was later hauled away from the scene by fellow Class 323 No. 323222.

Subsequent to the accident set No. 323221 performed a series of adhesion tests over the Redditch branch. ∎

Illustrations: Mike Concannon

Shepperton

During the early 1980s, a number of problems were identified on modern electric and diesel multiple unit stock with braking during poor rail adhesion periods. The problem, compounded by off-wheel braking which did not keep the wheel tread clean, led to some classes being blacked by the trade unions until an answer was found to the problem.

To assist engineers to understand the causes of wheel/rail slide in damp conditions and especially the leaf-fall season, the Strawberry Hill to Shepperton line on the Southern Region was used as a test track for different types of train mounted rail cleaning and modified braking systems.

One of these test programmes called for a Class 508 to operate over the short branch laying a slippery fluid onto the running rails at the same time as applying its brakes - the results of the reduced adhesion being monitored by scientific staff on board the train.

The tests were carried out at sufficient distance from the Shepperton terminal to eliminate any risk of an accident.

After the nightly tests were carried out, a rail cleaning train should have travelled over the line to remove any traces of adhesion inhibitor.

However, during the early morning of 21 April 1982, the cleaning up was not carried out satisfactorily and when the first passenger train of the day, the 06.34 from Waterloo approached Shepperton at normal speed, the driver applied his brakes but the slip inducing paste on the rails rendered them near useless.

The train shot through the station and crashed into the buffer stops, on impact the buffer stops, which were fitted to a concrete wall and an undertrack concrete plate, lifted and acted like a launch pad, raising the train over the station perimeter wall and leaving it hanging over the main road.

Athough the driver was shaken by his accident he was not injured, neither were the few passengers on the train.

This accident was the subject of a BR internal enquiry, which deemed that after any such adhesion inhibiting fluids have been laid on tracks for test purposes, the track must be properly cleaned and drivers of following trains warned that tests have been carried out and to drive with extra care.

The train came to land under the footbridge of the UKs leading transport publisher Ian Allan. ∎

Illustrations: CJM

Doncaster

West Yorkshire PTE green and cream liveried Class 141 'Pacer' No. 141116 was involved in a buffer stop collision in Doncaster West Yard in March 1986, while awaiting entry into Doncaster Works for attention.

At the time the unrefurbished set still had a Tightlock coupler, which during the impact wedged itself below the facia plate of the rail-built buffer stop.

Structural damage was minimal and the vehicle was pulled clear of the blocks and into the works by local staff.

This set was subsequently refurbished and renumbered to 141115. ■

Illustration: Derek Porter

Tonbridge

This little mess happened at Tonbridge East Yard on 15 November 1984, when the then yard shunter - a Class 08 - propelled a rake of vans destined for the main line into the yard and collided with the buffer stops, forcing three vans into derailment. ■

Illustration: Keith Dungate

Walton-on-Thames

Southern coach S66S was involved in a shunting runaway at Oatlands carriage sidings, Walton-on-Thames in summer 1966, with the coach ending up riding completely over the buffer stops and onto the end of the platform. The coach was condemned on site and broken up. ■

Illustration: CJM Collection

Saltley

Thankfully the viaduct wall at Saltley near Birmingham was a strong structure and withstood the impact of Class 45/0 'Peak' No. 45045 *Coldstream Guardsman*, which collided with force with the structure on 12 February 1983 while performing shunting duties at the nearby Lawley Street Freightliner terminal. The loco was recovered to Saltley depot and later taken to BREL Derby Works where a decision was taken to withdraw the locomotive. It was sold to Vic Berry of Leicester and broken up in November 1986.

It is understood that the driver involved in this incident became known as 'A bridge too far'! ∎

Illustration: Phil Cotterhill

Waterloo

This embarrassing incident occurred at Waterloo on 23 August 1975, when the author of this book was the secondman on the station pilot, a Class 09. During a shunting move to position vans carrying gold bullion from Southampton Docks (from South Africa) to Waterloo, the train, which was longer than the driver thought collided with the buffer stops in the dock platform, then located between platforms 11 and 12. The impact buffer locked the middle wagon, which also derailed.

Needless to say the authorities who had been sent to collect the bullion were seen scraping around the floor collecting any small traces of gold!

The accident was blamed on driver error! ∎

Illustration: CJM

The workshops at Crewe, from BR days through BREL, ABB to the present owner of Bombardier Transportation, have always been associated with the Brush Type 4, later Class 47 fleet. After building a substantial number of the fleet, the works took on the major overhaul and repair role, dealing with a huge number of collision repairs over the years. This spread shows just a small selection of locos which came to grief on the main line, with repair work nearly always requiring a replacement or heavily repaired cab.

Number D1684 (above), a Western Region-allocated loco appears to have had some heavy end contact, possibly through running into another train or a wagon. A repair such as this would require a new cab section from the rear of the cab door, plus new internal fittings.   No. D1591 (below), from the Swansea allocation was involved in a corner post collision at its No. 2 end in late 1964 and was repaired at Crewe. The drivers side received serious damage, as did the nose end with several body skin piercings. ■
Illustrations: CJM Collection

Introduced as D1948 and allocated to the London Midland Region - Western Lines, this loco had obviously received some quite serious frontal damage in this June 1967 view, which appears to have run into some form of obstruction, possibly another locomotive.

This loco was repaired with new cab front panels and was subsequently modified with electric train heat as No. 47505 and was later modified as one of the Edinburgh-Glasgow push-pull Class 47/7s as No. 47712.

The loco is still in service now operated by Direct Rail Service. ■
Illustration: CJM Collection

After receiving heavy buffer impact, which caused another vehicle to override into the front body of the Brush Type 4, No. D1843, later No. 47193 is seen in two-tone green livery at Crewe Works in mid-1967.

The heavy frontal impact broke off the heads of the buffers and depressed the bodywork inwards by some six inches. Note how the tail light housings are hanging out the bodywork. ∎
Illustration: CJM Collection

While allocated to Gateshead in the mid-1960s, No. D1578 was involved in a serious collision which destroyed the entire cab at the No. 2 end.

With obvious replacement buffers fitted and a limited amount of clean up work to bring the loco structure back into gauge, the loco is seen in Crewe Works yard awaiting stripping and a replacement cab section. EE Type 4 No. D248 in seen behind. ∎
Illustration: CJM Collection

The first of the standard Brush Type 4s No. D1521, which was later renumbered to 47001 is seen inside the shop at Crewe Works during an assessment following arrival with serious front end damage, in which it appears something has struck the front end mid-way up the windscreen and damaging the front end bodywork and handrails.

Major assessment of every loco admitted to works was required for costing and the ordering of replacement parts, with the records carefully filed in the technical details of the locomotive. ∎
Illustration: CJM Collection

Watford
23 January 1975

Locomotives:	83003, 86204, 86209
Stock:	Mk1
Trains:	22.15 Euston to Glasgow
	19.10 Manchester to Euston
Accident Type:	Collision after hitting debris on the track
Passengers:	150
Fatalities:	1
Injuries:	23

On 23 January 1975, the 20.12 company train from Ford Motors at Dagenham to Halewood powered by Class 85 No. 85017 forward from Willesden was formed of box vans loaded with stillages carrying engine transmission parts for new motor cars. On its way to Willesden for a change from diesel to electric power the train was stopped by signals at Gospel Oak, where robbers broke into the train thinking it was carrying saleable motor car parts. They left the wagons side doors open and might have dislodged the stillages. After gaining speed travelling north on the West Coast Main Line two of the stillages fell through the open door and landed on the up main line track on the approaches to Watford Junction.

Some 20 minutes later a very late running passenger train, the 19.10 Manchester Piccadilly to Euston after pulling away from its Watford Junction stop struck the two stillages, derailing and headed towards the down main line. The train was led by Class 83 No. 83003 piloting failed Class 86 No. 86204, the pilot engine had been attached at Macclesfield.

Seconds after the train became derailed, it was struck at speed by the 22.15 Euston to Glasgow sleeping car express powered by Class 86/2 No. 86209. The impact was corner post to corner post, the northbound train was deflected to the left in the direction of travel with the loco receiving only moderate damage and ending up down the embankment. The Class 83 was virtually sliced in two by the impact. Sadly the booked driver for the southbound train, who was riding on the secondmans side of the loco was killed instantly, the controlling driver sustained injuries but survived. The driver of the northbound train survived without serious injury.

A full inquiry was held into the accident under Department of Environment regulations and chaired by Lieut Col I. K. A. McNaughton, he found that the accident was caused by the southbound train striking an object on the

Above: *The virtually cut in half Class 83 No. 83003 which was piloting the southbound 19.10 Manchester Piccadilly to Euston train on 23 January 1975. It is no wonder that the driver riding on the non-driving side was killed and it is a miracle that the controlling driver was not killed as well.* CJM

track which had fell from a northbound freight service, which had its doors forced by train robbers at Gospel Oak.

Considerable comment was passed at the time about having company trains transporting potentially high-valued goods carrying business names, as this was considered to attract robbers to trains. The report also considers that better arrangements and methods of securing such trains be made and that locations where such

trains stop should be secure to reduce the risk of such incidents.

The two Class 86/2s involved in this accident were repaired at BREL Crewe and returned to service. The Class 83 was well beyond repair and was broken up. Most of the coaching stock was returned to use. ●

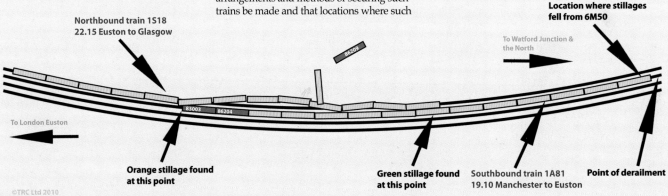

Northbound train 1S18
22.15 Euston to Glasgow

Location where stillages fell from 6M50

To Watford Junction & the North

To London Euston

Orange stillage found at this point

Green stillage found at this point

Southbound train 1A81
19.10 Manchester to Euston

Point of derailment

©TRC Ltd 2010

Above & Right: *The recovery of No. 86209 from the embankment was a very difficult operation. It was quickly decided that the only way out was by road, as it was impossible to haul the loco back up the embankment onto the railway. However, the ground in the area was very soft and a special roadway had to be built before recovery could be undertaken, which was not done until March. The view above shows two huge Sparrows road cranes lifting the body complete with bogies from the embankment prior to mounting on a road low loader for transport to Crewe. The view right shows the part sheeted loco laying on the embankment where it fell. Thankfully the embankment was soft after winter rain and did not cause undue damage to the underside of the loco. Both: CJM Collection*

Right: *After the Class 83 had been rerailed and some of the out of gauge bodywork removed, it was slowly hauled back towards Watford Junction station past the derailed coaches of the northbound sleeper train, thus allowing cranes to be brought in and recover the passenger stock. The passenger cars were all righted and rerailed and taken away by rail. The extent of the front end damage to the Class 83 can clearly be seen in this view. CJM Collection*

Level Crossing Accidents

Angmering

There are a high number of level crossing accidents in the UK, and these are mainly caused by the road user either trying to 'jump' the lights, skirt around half barrier crossings or drivers failing to carry out correct procedure for crossing the line at unprotected or occupation crossings.

However, this accident on the level crossing at the end of Angmering station on 16 May 1995 was caused by the 07.22 Brighton to Portsmouth Harbour formed of Class 421 4-CIG No. 1847 passing the protecting signal at danger and colliding with a light van crossing the tracks at the time. Thankfully the road vehicle driver survived his ordeal and only received a broken leg.

It was reported that the train had a brake problem which caused the train to overshoot the signal. ■

Illustrations: John A. M. Vaughan

Pooley Green

Incidents where road users dodge unmanned and unprotected crossings in the UK is on the increase and frequently have destructive and fatal results. During the early evening of 8 June 1984, the half-hourly Staines to Weybridge 'shuttle' formed of Class 412 2-EPB No. 5793 was approaching Pooley Green crossing near Egham, Surrey when just a few yards from the half barrier crossing a van hauling a broken down car tried to zig-zag around the lowered barriers. Although the train's driver slammed the brakes on he could not avoid a collision. The impact broke the van and trailer apart, with the train stopping some 200 yards down the line with the truck jammed under the wheels of the train.

The train's driver escaped without injury, but the two people in the road vehicle were killed. ∎

Illustration: CJM

Operation 'Zebra'

In 1994 Railtrack North west and the British Transport Police held 'Operation Zebra' to increase awareness of the risks of the incorrect use of public level crossings and launched a concerted attack on road users who misused crossings.

The 1994 campaign caught a staggering 345 road users breaking the law.

The culmination of 'Operation Zebra' was on 6 September 1994 when the BTP and Network Rail staged a deliberate level crossing accident as part of a nationwide TV advertising campaign.

The staging of the rail crash was a complex affair and was held at Yafforth on the mothballed Redmire branch near Northallerton.

Under the control of BR Research at Derby two former BR Southern region TC cars 977684 and 977687 which had recently been used for Channel Tunnel testing were coupled together. The test saw Class 47 No. 47981 haul the two TC cars between two barriers to a point 1,000 yards (305m) east of Yafforth where the rear barrier was detached to protect the ECML at Castle Hills Junction. The train then continued to near Ainderby from where the TCs cars were propelled towards a pre positioned Vauxhall Astra car straddling the line at Yafforth level crossing.

Using a slip coach to detach the TC unit, it collided with the motor vehicle at 36mph (58km/h) and pushed it some 175ft (54m) down the line before stopping, totally destroying the road vehicle and if people had been in the car they would not have survived. ∎

Illustration: CJM

Modern Traction Rail Mishaps - A pictorial study

Depot Mishaps and Problems

East Wimbledon

On 30 November 1984 a shunting accident occurred at East Wimbledon depot, when Class 455/8 No. 5864 collided with the buffer stops in the yard and demolished one of the depot lamp standards.

In the background two of the depots Class 508 sets Nos. 508026 and 508006 can be seen. ■

Illustration: Philip Cotterill

Doncaster

A not uncommon depot problem is where points are inadvertently moved under a vehicle with one bogie running down one track and the other bogie along a different line. The results can often be quite impressive, but a great embarrassment for the staff involved.

One such incident of this nature occurred at Doncaster West Yard in early 1981 when Class 110/1 DMC No. E52079 was being shunted. With both bogies still on the track, recovery was quite easy, with the vehicle retracing its previous 100ft (31m) of movement to regain the correct line. ■

Illustration: Derek Porter

Streatham Hill

Depot runaways, through trains being left without proper handbrakes applied were a common problem in the 1960-80s.

One on the Southern Region at Streatham Hill depot which provided this spectacular result was on 14 June 1980, when Class 427 4-VEG No. 7911 ran away from the shed and headed towards Streatham Junction colliding with the concrete buffer stop, climbing over the top with the DTC landing on its side straddling the slow line tracks and the MBSO ending up at an angle in front of the signalbox blocking both slow and one fast line.

Class 73 No. 73107 is seen with the Stewarts Lane crane, while the Brighton crane is in the background. ■

Illustration: Geoff Parkinson

Littlehampton

Movements around Littlehampton in West Sussex are normally well ordered and operate without problem. However on Sunday 6 November 1988, when Class 422 4-BIG No. 2205 was shunting it split a pair of facing points and the rear two vehicles tried to travel down a different line than the front two, resulting in the total derailment of the MBSO and partial derailment of the adjoining buffet car

The station of Littlehampton can be seen in the background. ■

Illustration: John A. M. Vaughan

Stewarts Lane

On the same day as Stewarts Lane was rolling out the first of its Electro Diesels No. 73123 in Gatwick Express livery, an inward empty stock move from Victoria to the electric multiple unit shed became derailed outside the depot offices.

The incident resulted in the rear bogie of Class 423 4-VEP No. 7864 dropping off the track. As Stewarts Lane was the base for the local recovery crane this was quickly fired up and put to use to re-rail the two wheelsets. The crane used was the then spare recovery crane No. ADRR95225 a 36 ton steam crane built by Ransomes & Rapier and originally numbered as DS80.

The derailment did not hinder the roll out of the Class 73 as this was thankfully inside the carriage works shed and it was possible to move it under diesel conditions to the coaching stock yard by the side of the EMU shed. ■

Illustration: CJM

Fairwater Yard

As the Track Renewal Train (TRT) hauled by Freightliner Heavy Haul Class 66/5 No. 66596 arrived back at its base in Taunton Fairwater Yard on 28 March 2009, a set of points on the reception road split under the moving train.

As the wagons tried to travel in different directions over pointwork, three became derailed, with one of the trains YJA wagons turning over onto its side with both bogies ripped off.

There was no obstruction of the main running lines and a normal service

continued without any delays.

Due to the location of the derailment it was impossible to use a road based crane to effect the required lift, therefore on 30 March the Margam-based rail recovery crane and tool vans arrived followed by the Toton-based crane and tool vans the following day.

It was planned to lift the wagon during a blockade of the main lines overnight on 31 March and 1 April 2009. However, while the equipment and site were being prepared on 31 March, the Toton-based crane No. ADRC 96715 struck a 132kV overhead power line at the southern end of the yard. This not only seriously damaged

the electrical systems of the crane, but also burnt out the Taunton area signalling and track circuit systems.

The lift was cancelled and major disruption was caused to train services before normal operations could be resumed early on 2 April 2009.

The Wigan-based crane was then summoned to replace the Toton crane, arriving on site on 2 April 2009.

The lift was eventually carried out overnight on Saturday and Sunday 4/5 April and the damaged Toton crane was eventually removed from the yard by road transport on 6 July 2009 for heavy repair.

The accident was caused by a track defect. The vehicle from the TRT which landed on its side was repaired by maker Plasser & Theurer at West Ealing. ■
Illustrations: Brian Garrett

Clapham Yard

Pullman cars used on the South Eastern and South Western sections of the Southern Region were maintained at Clapham Junction carriage and wagon shops.

On 5 August 1950, *Mimosa* became derailed at the entry of the yard with one bogie dropping off the track. Rerailing was achieved by the use of a local crane brought to the scene by Class 700 0-6-0 No. 30694.

Note the large group of on-lookers observing operations. ■

Illustration: G. R. Mortimer

Mottram Yard

Woodhead electric No. E26017 split the points during a shunting move in Mottram Yard between Hadfield and Broadbottom in June 1956.

The loco was rerailed by jacks, a far more convenient way of lifting a loco when overhead power lines are in use.

Note the tool van on the right in which the hydraulic jacks have been brought to the accident site, and the light traversing table, located below the loco. ■

Illustration: CJM Collection

Long Rock

The depot at Long Rock, Penzance, operated by First Great Western is used for servicing of HST stock and power cars as well as the sleeping car stock used on the Penzance to Paddington route.

On the morning of 25 June 2010 a depot shunt move went wrong, when an HST set split the points at the depot, resulting in Class 43 power car No. 43150 and adjoining TF No. 41133 derailing all wheels. The TF started the derailment by trying to traverse two roads at the same time, dragging the power car into derailment.

Recovery was undertaken by local staff using jacks. ■

Illustrations: Darren Harris.

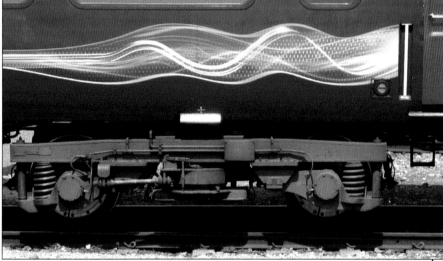

Stromeferry

While working the 15.23 Aberdeen to Kyle of Lochalsh on 18 November 2008, First ScotRail Class 158 No. 158723 struck a landslip approximately one mile from Stromeferry in Wester Ross.

The train was travelling at low speed and only the front bogie was derailed, none of the passengers or crew were injured. The line remained closed until 24 November while the sides of the cutting were stabilised. ■

Illustration: D. J. Henderson

Bedhampton

It is quite amazing just what can be repaired and returned to main line operation.

This is all that remained of Class 33/1 No. 33115 after it was involved in a collision with a track maintenance crane between Hilsea and Fratton on 25 February 1979.

The Class 33 was working with 4TC set No. 422 and forming the 01.35 Eastleigh to Portsmouth, when it struck a mobile crane at speed.

Remarkably the driver survived, but an off-duty guard who was travelling in the leading cab was sadly killed.

No. 33115 was later recovered to Fratton depot and several days later was transferred to the Southern Region accident repair facility at Slade Green in Kent and fully repaired, returning to traffic in mid-1980. ■

Illustration: CJM

Barrow upon Soar

On 1 February 2008, a tipper lorry delivering ballast to a Network Rail engineering site just to the north of Barrow upon Soar station struck a footbridge with it's raised body causing the bridge to collapse across the running lines.

The signaller was informed and all signals returned to danger, but shortly afterwards at 06.32 Class 158 No. 158856 forming the 06.13 Nottingham to Norwich service was unable to stop in time and collided with the fallen bridge deck while travelling at 65 mph (97km/h).

The train came to rest over 500 ft (152m) from the point of impact with the front bogie derailed and severe damage to the driver's cab.

The driver was trapped in his cab for more than three hours before being released and taken to hospital with leg injuries. He was released the following day.

The guard and one passenger were also taken to hospital but were released the same day.

Services were restored on the slow lines the following day while track repairs were carried out at the crash site. The ballast dropped by the lorry can be seen in the distance and the remains of the footbridge and its abutments can be seen beyond the road bridge. ■

Illustrations: Paul Biggs

Selby

Just after 06.00 on 28 February 2001 a Land Rover towing a trailer loaded with a Renault estate car was travelling along the M62 Motorway near Great Heck in South Yorkshire. The Land Rover veered off the motorway and went down an embankment onto the southbound track of the East Coast Main Line.

The Land Rover driver tried to reverse his vehicle off the track but was unable to do so, he then got out of the vehicle and contacted the emergency services using his mobile phone.

As he was speaking on the telephone at 06.14, the 04.45 Newcastle to London King's Cross formed of a GNER Mk4 set, with DVT No. 82221 leading and Class 91 No. 91023 propelling, travelling at a speed of 125mph

(201km/h), collided with the Land Rover. The leading bogie of the DVT derailed and the train continued in this state for some distance, but the points for the sidings at Great Heck deflected the DVT towards the opposite track. At the same time, Freightliner Heavy Haul Class 66/5 No. 66521 hauling the 05.50 Immingham to Ferrybridge Power Station loaded coal train, was travelling in the opposite direction at approximately 60mph (97 km/h).

The Class 66 struck the derailed DVT about half a mile from the location where the DVT had originally collided with the Land Rover and although the passenger train had slowed down, the combined impact speed was approximately 140mph (225km/h).

The DVT was virtually destroyed and all nine coaches of the train were damaged, some severely with many overturning down an embankment on the east side of the line,

the Class 91 was derailed but remained upright with only minor damage.

The Class 66 overturned onto its left hand side with major damage to its right hand side and cab area. Nine wagons derailed, several of which received major damage.

On the passenger train, the driver, guard and travelling chef were killed along with six passengers, 52 passengers were seriously injured. All of the fatalities and the majority of the serious injuries occurred in the front five coaches which included two first class vehicles and a restaurant car. These had lower density seating otherwise the injury toll could have been much worse. Total occupants of the passenger train was 99 passengers plus train crew, a low figure due to the early departure time of the train.

The driver of the Class 66 was killed but another crew member, also in the leading cab, survived.

The rescue operations at the scene were unusual as disinfecting procedures had to be carried out due to the foot and mouth epidemic which was ongoing at the time of the accident.

Class 66/5 No. 66521 despite only being a few months old at the time of the accident was written off. Most vehicles were recovered and taken to Bombardier Doncaster Works, the Class 66 was later stored at Leeds Midland Road Depot.

Class 66/5 No. 66526 was subsequently named *Driver Steve Dunn (George)* in tribute to No. 66521s driver who lost his life.

The Class 91, No. 91023 was the same locomotive which was involved in the Hatfield derailment on 17 October 2000 just a few months earlier. When the Class 91 fleet was upgraded all the locomotives had 100 added to their existing number, except for No 91023, which had the 23 reversed and became No. 91132.

EWS Class 56 No. 56115 was later named *Barry Needham* to commemorate an EWS

employee who was one of the passengers killed on the train.

The driver of the Land Rover claimed that he had either suffered a mechanical failure or struck an object in the carriageway. However, an investigation concluded that on examination the vehicle was not defective. It was concluded that the driver had not applied the brakes at any time when he went down the embankment but had been driving in a sleep-deprived state having been talking by telephone throughout all the previous night to a woman he had met on the internet.

He was subsequently charged with causing death by dangerous driving on 10 counts. He was found guilty at court on 13 December 2001 and sentenced to five years imprisonment but was released after serving two and a half years of his sentence.

Campaigners had claimed that there was an insufficient length of barrier at the bridge where the Land Rover had left the motorway, after the Health and Safety Executive's report had stated that the Land Rover had easily broken through a wooden fence some 24 metres before the crash barrier started. But in 2003 the Highways Agency review of crash barriers at bridges found that only three bridges nationwide needed to be upgraded and the bridge at Great Heck was not one of them. ■

Illustrations: Left, Above: Derek Porter, Right: Neil Daykin

Rickerscote

On Friday 8 March 1996 train 6M27 an air brake freight from Mossend Yard to Willesden Brent Yard via Bescot was headed by Class 37/0s Nos. 37071 and 37207.

Amongst its consist of 23 wagons were 13 two-axle 46 tonnes gross weight tank wagons carrying carbon dioxide gas in liquid form under pressure.

The train had passed over a lineside hot axle box detector at Great Bridgeford just north of Stafford at 22.25 and no problems

were detected. Shortly afterwards just south of Stafford station the train took the Birmingham line, diverging from the West Coast Main Line.

The Birmingham route directly after the junction consists of up fast, up slow and down fast tracks, the freight train signalled

onto the up fast and was accelerating away from the junction reaching a speed of between 30-35mph (48-56km/h), when shortly after passing the point where the up slow rejoins the up fast track, the driver realised his train had an emergency brake application.

As his train came to a stand, he saw train 1S09, the 21.40 Coventry to Glasgow Travelling Post Office (TPO) train hauled by Class 86/2 No. 86239 formed of nine Mk1, post and mail coaches pass him.

His freight train had come to a stand due to one of the tank wagons, No. STS53241, which was the ninth vehicle in the consist, suffering a total axle failure. It had been derailed for some distance and remained upright, but as it passed over the pointwork where the up slow and the up fast rejoined, the handbrake assembly and axleboxes which were now dragging at track level

jammed in the converging rails and caused the vehicle to derailed completely.

It broke free from the train and came to rest at right angles across the down fast line. The following 10 wagons also derailed with the last five remaining on the track but having extensive damage caused by buffer locking and overriding.

The mail train, which had been travelling at 90mph (145km/h) was slowing for the 60mph (97km/h) speed restriction for the junction with the West Coast Main Line.

The mail train driver would have seen the slow moving train but would have seen little of the wagon across the track as it was dark, giving him no time to make any sort of brake application and his train struck the derailed tank wagon at over 60mph (97km/h).

The Class 86 derailed on impact and turned onto its side, sliding along and up an embankment until it came to rest against the

end wall of a terraced house. The following four mail coaches came to rest in concertina fashion behind the locomotive with the following five coaches remaining upright and on the track.

The driver of the freight train walked back to inspect his train and find the reason for the brake application. On finding that his train had parted and that the catenary wires were down, he contacted the signaller to report that he believed there had been a collision and the emergency services were required.

Sadly one Post Office worker was killed and 19 rail staff including the Class 86 driver were injured.

Recover was a huge operation involving the use of two rail and two road cranes, with the line shut for more than a week. All the derailed mail vehicles together with the Res Class 86 were withdrawn and broken up. ∎

Illustrations: Mike Concannon

Birketts Common

The Settle & Carlisle line was the scene of a fatal accident during the evening of 31 January 1995, when the 16.26 Carlisle to Leeds and following 17.45 Carlisle to Leeds collided at Birketts Common.

The first southbound train was stopped from proceeding at Blea Moor due to flooding on the line ahead at Stainforth, the train crossed over tracks and was returning north to Kirkby Stephen to detrain its passengers. On its return journey north, it hit a landslip and derailed, with the leading coach veering into the path of the southbound track.

The derailed train's driver used his cab radio to report the incident, but the signalling centre could not communicate with the driver of the approaching southbound train, Class 156 No. 156468 forming the 17.45 Carlisle to Leeds, which by this time had departed from Kirkby Stephen, due to the terrain in the area.

It was a further seven minutes before the 17.45 Carlisle-Leeds approached the derailed train, with no possible way of advising the driver of what was ahead. The train struck the derailed vehicle at 45mph (72km/h), causing extensive damage to both leading vehicles.

The guard of the derailed train, rail enthusiast Stuart Wilson, was helping move passengers and their luggage to the rear coach of the train when the impact occurred and was sadly killed.

All four Class 156 vehicles were removed from the scene to Derby Litchurch Lane works and repaired.

The illustration left shows the damage sustained to the derailed vehicle from set No. 156490 after recovery to Derby Litchurch Lane. ■

Illustration: CJM

Sough Tunnel

On Sunday 22 March 1981, the 07.40 Manchester Victoria to Blackburn service, formed of Class 108 vehicles Nos. 52059 and 51945 collided with a landslip at the western portal of the 1 mile 255 yard (1,842m) long Sough Tunnel between Entwistle and Darwen

The train was only travelling at low speed with the front coach and leading bogie of the second vehicle derailing.

The weather at the time was cold and snowy with the waterlogged embankment giving out and landing up on the tracks.

The train was rerailed by jacks and line reopened the following day after embankment stablisation. ■

Illustration: Mark Radnedge

West Ealing

On Sunday 6 August 1989, the 21.15 'Network Express' from Oxford to Paddington was derailed at West Ealing by obstructions placed on the track near Hanwell, earlier in the day other obstructions had been removed and it was believed that the same persons were involved.

Class 50 No. 50025 *Invincible* powering the train struck the object on the track and pushed it along for nearly a mile until it struck a set of points on the approach to West Ealing station. The loco toppled onto its side and slid along the track and onto the platform edge, fortunately the robustness of the Mk2 passenger coaches saw them remain upright and did not foul the path of an HST which passed the wrecked train on an adjacent track seconds after the accident.

After the derailment a small fire broke out on the locomotive and damaged some of the stock.

Seven people, including the driver, were treated for shock and minor injuries.

Recovery of the train was carried out by staff from Old Oak Common, who used a mix of rail and road cranes to effect a lift. No. 50025 was taken out by road from the car park of an adjacent supermarket and taken to Old Oak Common.

The loco was subsequently withdrawn and broken up at Old Oak Common. ■

Illustrations: Top/Middle: Brian Morrison
Bottom: CJM

Mottingham

On the morning of 11 October 1977 a Welbeck Colliery to Northfleet cement works Merry-go-Round (MGR) coal train headed by a pair of Class 47s came to a stand near Mottingham on the Hither Green to Dartford line. The driver failed to control the train through correctly applying the brakes and it rolled back a short distance.

The slight rolling back, caused two of the MGR wagons to derail on a set of catchpoints and become foul of the adjacent up running line.

Class 33/0s No. 33043 and 33036 were at the same time heading the 03.24 Northfleet cement works to Dunstable cement train formed of bogie wagons in the opposite direction, this train struck the derailed wagons and immediately became derailed.

No. 33043 remained at track level but No. 33036 and several cement wagons plunged down the embankment and landed in gardens of houses next to the line.

A massive clear up operation was arranged, with the cement hoppers at rail height being rerailed and removed with the aid of two steam cranes. The Class 33 down the embankment took nearly seven weeks to recover. It was uprighted by road cranes and separated from its bogies before being lifted by two rail cranes up the embankment and onto the rail system.

The loco was transferred to Slade Green where repairs were considered but these were not authorised and the loco was cut up nearly two years later.

No. 33043 was repaired and returned to traffic. ■

Illustration: Left CJM
Below: Brian Morrison

Cruachan

On the evening of 6 June 2010 the 18.20 First ScotRail service from Glasgow Queen Street to Oban, collided with fallen rocks in the Pass of Brander near the Falls of Cruachan.

The train was formed of Class 156 No. 156499. The leading vehicle DMSL No. 52499 rode over the rocks causing it to derail and was only prevented from crashing down the embankment to the road below by lineside trees. Although extensive damage was caused to the leading vehicle there were only minor injuries to eight people on board. The train was carrying 60 passengers and three crew at the time of the accident.

West Coast Railway Co Class 37/5 No. 37676 recovered DMS vehicle No. 57499 from the scene but recovery of the DMSL proved to be far more problematic. A long reach 1,000 tonnes capacity crane belonging to Ainscough was used. As the A85 road adjacent to the accident scene was on a viaduct over Loch Awe at this point, the crane had to be positioned further back on the solid part of the road.

The Loch also had to be protected with oil booms to prevent pollution should there be a spill of fuel or oil during the lift.

Recovery of the DMSL vehicle was completed on 11 June 2010, with both vehicles being taken to Glasgow Works for assessment.

The Oban line was closed for a total of eight days while the lift and repairs took place reopening on Monday 14 June 2010. ■

Illustrations: Donald Stirling

Lavington

On 10 July 2010 power car No. 43041 leading the 13.06 Paddington to Penzance struck a fallen tree on the Berks & Hants route near Lavington.

The train struck the tree at approximately 90mph (145km/h) causing extensive damage to the cab with the tree becoming lodged within the cab. An emergency brake application was made by the driver, but the collision could not be avoided. The tree destroyed some of the electrical equipment and the anti-wheel slide system failed, with the train continuing for some considerable distance with all wheels locked and serious wheel flats were caused throughout the train.

After the tree was removed from the cab and the driver taken to hospital, the train was hauled forward to Westbury by Class 59/2 No. 59201 at 5mph (8km/h) due to the severe wheel flats.

The train eventually arrived at Westbury some five hours late, where passengers were transferred to another HST for their onward journey.

Following examination at Westbury the rear power car No. 43135 hauled the complete train to St. Phillips Marsh HST Depot in the early hours of Monday 12 July 2010 at a maximum speed of 5mph (8km/h).

Thankfully the driver only received minor injuries which shows just how strong the HST cabs actually are. ∎

Illustrations: Mark Few

Annan

On 15 March 1976 Class 47/0 No. 47274 hauling the 20.55 Euston to Stranraer overnight sleeper train collided with a lorry that had crashed onto the line from a bridge at Annan between Gretna and Dumfries. Both members of the loco crew and the lorry driver were killed.

The lorry driver was found to have three times the permissible amount of alcohol in his blood.

After this accident new regulations were introduced regarding barriers adjacent to bridges where the railway was at risk. ■
Illustration: K. S. McQuade

Ashchurch

Hymek Type 3 No. D7038 is seen stabled at Ashchurch, Gloucestershire in March 1969 with serious front end and side damage following hitting a door on a freight wagon.

The loco was repaired at Swindon and returned to service later the same year. ■
Illustration: Norman E. Preedy

Wichnor

DMMU car No. M59322 from a three-car set is seen in a field at Wichnor (Staffs) following impact with a tractor on a level crossing, while working a Birmingham to Derby service in January 1969. ■
Illustration: John Tuffs

Copmanthorpe

Moor Lane, Copmanthorpe south of York is the site of a former level crossing, which closed in 1982.

On the evening of 25 September 2006 a car crashed through the fence and came to rest with its front wheels on the nearest track. About a minute later the 14.25 Virgin service from Plymouth to Edinburgh formed of Class 221 No. 221136 struck the car.

It was dark at the time with some fog and drizzle falling and although the train driver applied the emergency brake there was no time to decelerate before impact, which was at 100mph (161km/h).

Parts of the car passed under the train causing wheelsets two, three and four to derail on the front vehicle. The train remained upright and came to rest 907 metres past the point of impact. Nobody on the train was injured but the car driver was killed. ∎

Illustrations: Richard Armstrong

Surbiton

On Sunday 4 July 1971 a crash between a ballast train and passenger service occurred at Surbiton on the SR main line to Woking.

A ballast train, working from St Margarets to Farnham via Clapham Junction to run around was powered by Class 73s Nos. E6025 and E6033, somewhere between Clapham and Surbiton the 24th and 25th wagons became buffer locked and on approaching Surbiton station became derailed, veering in front of the 09.50 Waterloo to Portsmouth train formed of 4-VEP sets Nos. 7714 and 7806, which hit the derailed wagons at 72mph (116km/h).

The leading VEP coach from set No. 7714 turned over on its side, and during the impact one of the wagons broke the motor of a set of facing points sending several of the wagons into side swipe collision with the passenger train.

Amazingly nobody was killed in this incident, but the damage was massive, the lines through Surbiton being blocked for three days while cranes from Wimbledon and Eastleigh dealt with the wreckage. ■

Illustrations: CJM

Diesel Hydraulics and Swindon Works

The iconic workshops at Swindon, the centrepiece of Great Western Railway operations was the sole major workshop which dealt with the various ill-fated diesel-hydraulic fleets, while smaller facilities such as Newton Abbot Works dealt with some work, any collisions or major component exchanges were always undertaken at Swindon.

From photographic records it seems that the diesel-hydraulic classes were involved in more than their fair share of collisions and derailments, with each one documented and recorded. The illustrations on the next three spreads show some of the more interesting repairs which Swindon had to deal with over the hydraulic era. ■

Left: North British Type 4 B-B 'Warship' No. D846 **Steadfast** *poses in the yard at Swindon on 24 October 1966 after arriving with serious front end damage, which had totally distorted the nose end and destroyed all the buffer beam equipment.* **CJM Collection**

Below: After diesel hydraulic locos arrived at Swindon Works with serious collision damage a major assessment of required repairs was undertaken, followed by a costing. These were then reviewed and authorisation given to effect a repair. Obviously the minimum downtime possible was sought, as a loco laying around the workshops was not earning money. NBL Type 2 No. D6322 is seen inside the main shop during its assessment period on 13 February 1967. **CJM Collection**

Right & Below: *After reportedly being involved in a freight train collision with low bodied wagons, No. D1049* **Western Monarch** *stands between the main workshop building and the main line after arriving for repair on 20 March 1969. Note the cut along the bottom of the bodyside where obviously either a vehicle or structure had cut into the usually strong body skin like a knife.*
CJM Collection

Left & Below: *In March 1969, Class 35 'Hymek' No. D7038 was involved in an accident near Ashchurch, Gloucestershire, when it collided with an open wagon door, sustaining serious front end and side collision damage. After recovery from the accident scene, the loco was towed to Swindon and is viewed inside 'A' shop on 18 March 1969 awaiting cleaning up, removal of the front end and fitting a new cab section. Note in the background of the upper picture, Brush prototype Falcon No. D0280 can be seen.* CJM Collection

Right: Few serious accidents befell the five North British prototype 'A1A-A1A 'Warship' locos. However, this view of No. D604 Cossack has come to light showing significant cab end and side damage, with the side skirt ripped off and the later applied right side section of the two-character headcode display totally missing. This illustration was captioned as being taken inside the weigh shop, so it was likely that the loco was being stored at this location either awaiting or during its assessment period.
CJM Collection

Below: After being cut open like a tin can, North British 'Warship' No. D835 Pegasus awaits entry into the main workshop at Swindon in 1967. Reports indicate this loco collided with a derailed freight wagon.
CJM Collection

Front ends are always the most likely part of a loco to receive collision damage. In the upper left view we seen the front of 'Western' No. D1071, while top right is the cab end of 'Warship No. D846. Below left we see BR rail blue liveried 'Warship' No. D833 **Panther**, the first of the North British B-B locos, inside 'A' shop at Swindon after suffering major side swipe damage, which was likely caused by the loco either passing or being passed by another loco or train on converging point work. The view bottom right shows the B end of 'Hymek' No. D7048, which received serious front and side damage in a roll over accident. This loco sports the early BR blue with small yellow warning panel livery.
All: CJM Collection

Above: Following a derailment at Spetchley in early July 1969, in which 'Hymek' No. D7048 ended up on its side, the locomotive received very serious front end and side damage. Many thought the loco would be withdrawn, but the expertise of the bodyshop at Swindon Works returned the loco to front line use, remaining active until 1972. This view taken on 24 July 1969 shows the loco after recovery from the crash site and stabled at Swindon awaiting assessment. Note the grass attached to the bodywork just to the right of the radiator side grille.
CJM Collection

Right: Green small yellow warning panel-liveried No. D7068 is seen inside Swindon 'A' shop on 6 June 1966 being stripped after arriving with serious front end damage after hitting a lineside obstruction. Note all the cables protruding from the front end, together with missing draw hook and buffers.
CJM Collection

The Results of Runaways

Kingsbury

On 6 August 1987, Railfreight Class 58 No. 58013 ran away driverless on the Kingsbury Colliery line and headed towards the main line.

As the loco approached the junction with the main line it derailed and landed up next to the main tracks.

After recovery the loco was taken to Toton depot and stored, providing spares for other class members until repairs were authorised in April 1988. The loco returned to traffic in June 1988 and is currently one of the fleet working for ETF on high speed line construction in France. ■

Illustration: Scott Borthwick

It was red faces on the Dartmoor Railway in late December 2008 when the line's 'Hampshire' unit No. 205028 ran away and derailed on catch points protecting the main line to Crediton.

The units DMBS ended up leaning at 45deg to its non-driving side, with the railway sticking tape over the number to try and hide its identity.

The set was recovered and repaired and is now frequently used on the Meldon-Okehampton route. ■

Illustration: Nathan Williamson

Meldon Quarry

On the evening of 12 September 2000, train 6A20 from Whatley Quarry to Acton Yard, loaded Mendip aggregate train derailed at 23.20 on the single-track branch line from the quarry on the exit from Great Elm tunnel.

The powering locomotive Class 59/1 No. 59103 *Village of Mells* overturned onto its left side and came to rest embedded in the parapet of a bridge over a small stream.

Several of the following wagons went into derailment with one ending up embedded in the rear of the locomotive.

Due to the limited access and terrain at the site recovery was very difficult, it was first thought that the locomotive might have to be cut up in situ, but it was eventually righted on 19 September 2000 and taken

Great Elm

back to Whatley Quarry. It was then removed from there by road to the EDU at Derby for assessment and later transferred to Eastleigh works where it was repaired and returned to service. ■

Illustrations: Mark Few

Carrbridge

On the first day following take over of the service by DB Schenker, the 13.14 Inverness to Mossend Yard service on Monday 4 January 2010 for Stobart Rail was hauled by recently re-painted Class 66/0 No. 66048 *James the Engine*.

At around 16.03 whilst descending the 1:60 grade on the single line from Slochd Summit, the train failed to stop at a red signal on the approach to Carrbridge station and continued for another 547yds (500m) before entering the loop line and through trap points.

While still travelling at around 60mph (96km/h) the loco and first wagon overshot the end of the run out track and came to rest in trees at the bottom of the embankment, close to houses.

The next five wagons of the train derailed and came to rest at varying angles across the loop and running line. The last four wagons of the train did not derail.

The driver and a technician travelling in the cab received minor injuries. The accident caused major damage to the railway infrastructure and it was sometime before services were restored.

Several of the trees around the locomotive had to be felled and hard standing laid so that a large road crane could gain access. It was exactly eight weeks to the day before No. 66048 was eventually removed from the scene. It was taken by road to Inverness before transfer by rail to Toton for assessment.

Evidence suggests that the braking performance of the train was below that expected of a train of this type. The weather at the time of the accident was poor, with a layer of snow over the railhead, heavy falling snow with extreme freezing temperatures. ■

Illustrations: Top & Left: Donald Stirling
Below: Jim Ramsey

BR Derby Type 2, later Class 25 No. D7623 ran away on the Nith Valley Line while powering a loaded coal train on 30 January 1967.

The train eventually derailed at Auchinleck causing severe damage to a number of 16 Ton mineral wagons, with the locomotive ending up an a 45 deg angle

Auchinleck

towards the drivers side and sustaining moderate damage. The loco was repaired at Derby Works and returned to traffic. ■

Illustration: Derek Cross

Severn Sisters

EWS-liveried, DBS-owned HTA bogie coal hopper No. 310200 was photographed at Severn Sisters on the Onllwyn branch in South Wales on 5 June 2010.

It was hit by run-away wagons from the Onllwyn washery and virtually destroyed by the impact.

To keep trains running and the line open, the damaged written-off wagon was lifted to the side of the line to await disposal. ■

Illustration: Darren Harris

Rear end Collisions and Derailments

East Croydon

At 01.23 on Saturday 16 January 1982, the 00.22 Three Bridges to New Cross Gate engineer's train formed of six wagons hauled by Class 73/1 No. 73115 ran into the rear of a stationary mail and parcels train standing in East Croydon station.

The parcels train was formed of nine bogie vans headed by Class 73/0 No. 73006.

The rear three vans of the mail train were derailed and severely damaged, as was the leading third of No. 73115.

The guard travelling in the rear cab of the engineer's train locomotive received slight injuries along with six post office staff working at the mail train together with a member of the platform staff.

The driver of the engineer's train was trapped in his cab for some time and received severe leg injuries. The line remained closed until 22.30 the following night.

The cause of the accident was the engineer's train passing a signal at danger and the inquiry concluded that as there was no fault with the signalling system, the blame lay with the driver who was either asleep or distracted from his duties. ∎

Illustration: John A. M. Vaughan

Wimbledon

On 12 October 1972 the 18.42 Acton to Wimbledon West coal train was hauled by Class 73/0 No. E6001 and formed of 22 wagons and a brake van loaded with coal and coke, with a combined train weight of 544 tons. The first six wagons formed a fitted head, the rest of the train was unbraked.

The train passed a signal at danger approaching the station and collided with the rear of the 19.05 Holborn Viaduct to West Croydon service formed of 4 EPB No. 5220, which was standing in platform 10 at Wimbledon station.

An enquiry found that the driver of the freight had become distracted and passed the distant signal showing yellow without seeing it. On the approach to Wimbledon station it was too late to stop in time. The impact was between 20-30mph (32-48km/h). The freight train driver and 11 passengers were injured. ∎

Illustration: CJM

Battersea Park

The robustness of the Mk2 passenger coach was brought into question following a rear end collision at Battersea Park on 31 May 1985. A Gatwick Express set was involved in a rear-end collision, and the impact was such that it broke the back of Class 488/3 vehicle No. 76200 from set No. 488301, just above the bogie centre pin.

The train was recovered by staff from Stewarts Lane with set No. 488301 being withdrawn. The damage can clearly be seen in this view at the accident site with the M&EE department staff trying to sheet over the damage before transfer to Stewarts Lane. The vehicle was broken up by staff at Stewarts Lane in July 1986. ■
Illustration: CJM

Norton Bridge

Over night on 15/16 October 2003 in connection with the West Coast Route Modernisation Project only one track was open between Norton Bridge and Crewe rather than the normal four.

At 03.00 an emergency possession was taken closing this track as well. A northbound Freightliner service the 21.15 Grain to Trafford Park powered by Class 66/5 No. 66534 came to a stand at 03.08 at the signal protecting the possession and as the driver of this train was speaking to the signalman on the telephone from the cab, his train was struck in the rear by the following Freightliner service, the 21.54 Ipswich to Trafford Park, powered by Class 86/6s Nos. 86631 and 86611 which was travelling at approximately 20 mph (32km/h) at the point of impact, causing severe structural damage to both locomotives which were subsequently withdrawn.

The driver was trapped in his cab, but on release was found to be largely uninjured.

The following enquiry found that the cause of the accident was that signal NB149 had been passed at danger by the driver of the following train with an overrun of 587 yards before impact.

Recovery was undertaken jointly by Freightliner, EWS and Network Rail. No. 86631, the most seriously damaged loco was lifted out by crane and taken to Bombardier Crewe by road, No. 86611 was re-bogied on site and taken to Stafford by rail and thence to Crewe. The local tracks at Norton Bridge were blocked for four days. ■
Illustrations: Andy Fudge

Newton Abbot

While the 07.20 Penzance to Edinburgh Waverley InterCity CrossCountry service was stationary at Newton Abbot station on 25 March 1994 with power car No. 43071 at the rear, the train was rammed by the following 09.40 Paignton to Cardiff service formed of a Class 158 DMU No. 158833.

The collision occurred at around 10-15mph (16-24km/h), when the driver of the Class 158 failed to stop on the protecting red signal located between Aller Divergence and Newton Abbot station. By the time he rounded the corner approaching the station it was too late to avoid a collision.

Recovery of the trains was undertaken by staff from Laira depot and consisted of pulling the two trains apart as no physical derailment had occurred. The HST power car was repaired at Crewe Works and the Class 158 at Derby Litchurch Lane.

A total of 35 passengers and staff were injured, none seriously.

It is interesting to note from the illustrations the strength of the Class 158 front end and that most of the damage to the HST was cosmetic. ∎

Illustrations: CJM

Bricklayers Arms Junction

Very few head-on collisions occur on the UK rail system, but one with catastrophic results occurred on 9 November 1975 at Bricklayers Arms Junction.

The 09.42 London Bridge to New Cross Gate empty stock train formed of eight Mk1s powered by Class 33/0 No. 33041, collided head on with the 09.02 Epsom Downs to London Bridge formed of 4-SUB No. 4704 at Bricklayers Arms Junction.

The accident was caused by the empty stock train passing the subsidiary signal at danger. In the official enquiry the driver was not held responsible for the accident as the sunlight reflecting off the front of the locomotive gave a clear impression that the two white lights of the subsidiary signal were illuminated.

The trains involved were recovered to New Cross Gate sidings. The Class 33 and SUB unit were withdrawn. ∎

Illustrations: CJM Collection

Motherwell

Class 85 No. 85031 hauling a northbound air brake fitted limestone train on 19 June 1979, was routed into the down Braidhurst Loop at Lesmahagow Junction, Motherwell. Unfortunately the loop line was already occupied by a stationary mixed freight train.

By the time the Class 85 driver had seen the train ahead, even though he made an emergency brake application it was too late to avert a collision at around 15mph (24km/h).

The damage was considerable, with the rear wagons of the stationary freight being thrown off the track, damaging the front of the loco, while several of the limestone hoppers overturned spilling their load over the adjoining running lines. The Motherwell-based brakedown train effected recovery. The Class 85 was subsequently repaired at BREL Crewe. ∎

Illustration: Lindsay Brown

Lawrence Hill

Train 1V04, the 16.35 Shieldmuir to Bristol Parkway Royal Mail Terminal arrived at its destination in the early hours of Wednesday 1 November 2000, running some three hours late hauled by Class 67 No. 67012 and formed of eight mail vans.

Due to adverse weather conditions, the train had been diverted via Chepstow and Newport, where the locomotive ran-round its train. This meant that the locomotive was now on the wrong end of the train for the empty stock working from Bristol Parkway Royal Mail hub to the EWS depot at Bristol Barton Hill where it was due for servicing.

Therefore, Class 67 No. 67002 *Special Delivery* was sent light from Bristol Barton Hill to haul the train back to the depot, operating in a 'top and tail' formation.

Shortly after 03.30 the train departed the RM terminal and while descending Filton bank the driver made a brake application for a red signal approaching Lawrence Hill. Even with a full emergency brake application there was no braking action whatsoever on the train, and while travelling at around 50mph (80km/h) the train collided in Lawrence Hill station with the rear of a slow moving 02.30 Avonmouth to Didcot Power Station loaded MGR coal train which was negotiating Dr Days Junction. The MGR was hauled by Class 60 No. 60072 *Cairn Toul*, which had been diverted from its normal route due to flooding in Chipping Sodbury tunnel.

In the collision Class 67 No. 67002 rode up over the last two wagons of the MGR train and came to rest on top of the third from last

wagon HAA No. 352154 and stopped with the locomotive cab against the parapet of the A420 Bristol to Chippenham road overbridge.

The first mailvan in the train, NIA No. 94533 was left at an angle pointing into the air and resting on the last wagon HMA No. B354618, while the fuel tank from No. 67002 was lying on the track underneath it.

The local brigade quickly extinguished a small fire, which had broken out within the wreckage.

No. 67002 was only nine months old at the time and received extensive damage to its bogies, underframe and cab ends. It was out of service for a considerable time, eventually being rebuilt at Crewe Works.

The line through Lawrence Hill was re-opened for operation at 06.15 on 3 November 2000.

The subsequent investigation found that with the train working in 'top and tail mode' the Brake Pipe Pressure Control Unit Isolating Cock on the rear Class 67 had not been closed. This meant that every time the driver in the front locomotive applied the train brakes the rear locomotive would create air pressure and release the brakes.

A number of revisions were subsequently made into driver training and instructions when operating trains with locomotives at both ends. ■

Illustrations: L. D. Merchant
Above: Ken Brunt

Winsford

A pair of Class 142 'Pacer' units Nos. 142003 and 142008 were returning to Manchester from Crewe as empty stock after tyre turning on 23 June 1999.

At Winsford South Junction where the quadruple West Coast Main Line reverts to double track, the Class 142s travelling over the down slow line failed to stop at the red signal protecting the converging junction.

The units ran through the points and came to a stand on the down track, the driver immediately sent a National Radio Network (NRN) radio message stating that he had passed a red signal and had come to a stand on the main line and asked for all trains in the Winsford area to stop.

The message was broadcast but Class 87/0 No. 87027 *Wolf of Badenoch* hauling the 06.30 Virgin Train's London Euston to Glasgow service formed of eight Mk3 coaches and a Driving Van Trailer was already approaching the scene and too close to stop.

The Class 87 driver made an emergency brake application when he saw the signal protecting the junction suddenly turn to red in front of him.

However, the Class 87 collided with the rear of unit No. 142008 at an estimated speed of 50mph (80km/h) causing considerable damage and shifting the body of the Class 142 unit from its underframe by around 7ft (2 metres). 27 people were injured in the collision four of which received serious injuries but it could have been much worse had not one of the trains been an empty stock working.

Recovery was undertaken by rail and road cranes with the Class 87 being taken to Crewe Works where it was fully repaired. The most damaged Class 142 was subsequently taken to Doncaster Works where it was condemned. ■

Illustrations: Mark Barber

Invergowrie

Class 25 No. 25083 hauling the 08.44 Glasgow Queen Street to Dundee stopping service formed of five coaches on 22 October 1979 had been having problems with loss of power during the journey.

On leaving the station stop at Invergowrie, the brakes on the leading bogie started binding and as the train ran alongside Invergowrie Bay the secondman reported to the driver that one of the traction motors was on fire. The train was then brought to a an immediate halt.

The following train, the 09.35 Glasgow Queen Street to Aberdeen hauled by Class 47/0 No. 47208 formed of seven coaches had been brought to a stand at Longforgan signal box home signal and then cleared forward to the starting signal which was at danger due to the preceding train still being in section.

The train continued to draw forward towards the home signal but then began to accelerate past it, the signalman noted that the signal was still at danger. The train continued to accelerate and passed through Invergowrie station at about 70mph (113km/h) at which point the stationary train ahead would have become visible.

An emergency brake application was made, but No. 47208 ran into the stationary Dundee train at an estimated speed of 60mph (97km/h).

The force of the impact catapulted the rear two coaches of the Dundee train over the sea wall and into the muddy banks of the River Tay, fortunately the tide was out at the time.

The driver and secondman of the Aberdeen train and two passengers on the Dundee train were killed instantly and a further passenger died of their injuries later, a total of 51 people were also injured.

Although it will never be known why the Aberdeen train passed the home signal at danger, several witnesses gave evidence that the home signal arm was not properly horizontal, being slightly raised by about eight degrees and the elevation which appeared to increase the closer one got to it.

Examination of the signal showed that the post bracket was badly bent and it was concluded that a chain from a passing wagon or engineer's machinery working by the lineside might have damaged it.

Also there was no AWS at the home signal, which if fitted would have given the driver a further warning that the signal was at danger. ■

Illustrations: Alex Coupar

Clapham

What became known as the Clapham rail disaster was a serious accident involving two collisions between three Network SouthEast commuter trains at 08.10 on Monday, 12 December 1988.

The collisions occurred 875 yards (800m) on the south west side of Clapham Junction station. Sadly 35 people died and 500 were injured, making the incident one of the worst in the UK in recent times.

The first collision occurred after the driver of the 07.18 Basingstoke to Waterloo saw a signal in front of him change from green to red. The driver stopped his train at the next signal post telephone to report the incident to Clapham Junction 'A' signal box. He was told there was no fault and that it was alright to proceed.

As the driver was returning to his train, it was hit from behind by a following train at between 35-40mph (56- 64 km/h), by the late-running 06.14 from Poole, running under a false clear signal.

A second collision, involved the second, third and fourth coaches of an empty train from Waterloo to Farnham, travelling south on the down main line, this hit the wreckage of the up Poole train, causing derailment and separation of the first carriage.

A fourth train approaching on the up main line, also running under false clear signals, managed to stop about 70 yds (60 m) from the rear of the already crashed Poole train.

The immediate cause of the accident was incorrect wiring work in which an old cable, wrongly left in place after rewiring work and still connected, created a false feed to a signal relay, thereby allowing its associated signal to show a green aspect when it should have been showing red.

The most significant cause of the accident was the failure by BR senior management to recognise that the Clapham area resignalling, covering all the lines out of Waterloo, should have been treated as a major, safety-critical project, controlled throughout by a single, senior, named project manager. Instead the job was left to middle-level technical staff, poorly supervised. Staffing levels were also inadequate and the staff generally depressed by months of voluntary seven-days-a-week work, were carrying out the complete resignalling of the busiest junction and area on the BR system.

British Rail were forced to overhaul their signal works testing regime.

The inquiry into the Clapham rail crash, chaired by Anthony Hidden QC, also recommended the introduction of the Automatic Train Protection (ATP) equipment; however the inquiry's recommendation was not acted on. Subsequent crashes at locations such as Southall in 1997 and Ladbroke Grove in 1999 could have been averted if ATP had been fully installed, these led to further recommendations for the introduction of ATP, and although it has been installed on some lines, it has not to date been specified for the entire UK rail network.

A memorial marking the location of the crash site is atop the embankment above the railway at Spencer Park, Windmill Road, Battersea. ■

Illustrations: Jeremy De-Souza

Newton Abbot

6 March 1997

Locomotive:	43130/LA11/43170
Stock:	HST
Train:	15.35 Paddington to Penzance
Accident Type:	Derailment
Passengers on train:	280
Fatalities:	0
Injuries:	6

More than 120 passengers had a lucky escape on 6 March 1997, when the 15.35 Paddington to Penzance train, formed of an HST set derailed on the approaches to Newton Abbot station.

The derailment began with the inner end of the second passenger coach from the front, which damaged the track to allow all following vehicles to go into derailment, the rear power car was derailed by only its inner bogie.

The train was formed of Class 43 No. 43130, coaching stock set LA11 and power car No. 43170 on the rear.

The design of the Mk3 passenger coach, assisted by the use of buck-eye couplings saw that the vehicles remained basically upright and in line, although some wheelsets dug into the ballast formation, digging up both down and up lines.

Some 200 yards (183m) after initial derailment, the trailing end of the second vehicle and the leading end of the third coach slewed over the up line, splitting the buck-eye couplers, this action also broke the air pipe which applied the trains brakes.

As the train was slowing to a stand, the second coach rode up over the central girder of the River Teign bridge and came to rest perched precariously on top.

Emergency services in the Newton Abbot and Torbay area were put on full alert as initially casualty figures were thought to be high, but in reality only six people were injured.

An initial inspection of the site on the evening of the crash decided that rail cranes could not be used in the recovery as the track was damaged in the area where lifting was needed. Three high-capacity road cranes were therefore hired for the recovery operation, with railway engineers and railway tool vans in attendance.

Under the control of the recovery team from EWS Cardiff Canton, assisted by staff from Laira the operation commenced at 09.00 on 7 March. The rear power car was first to be rerailed and taken to Exeter and then St Phillips Marsh for inspection.

The two FOs, the buffet cars and four TSOs were difficult to recover, requiring the use of two road cranes to make a lift and position in a siding of Hackney Yard. Cranes also had to be repositioned during each lift making the operation a lengthy affair.

The buffet car took more than three hours to recover due to its position and the risk of it toppling over.

The leading power car did not derail and was hauled to Laira and returned to traffic. The cause of the accident was the failure of the wheel bearing at the inner end of the leading TSO, the vehicle which ended up straddling the Teign Bridge. The axle journal was cut off by a sharp section of the bearing which led to the collapse of the bogie.

All vehicles except the leading TGS were removed from the scene by road, being loaded onto road trailers positioned at the rear of Newton Abbot racecourse. Repairs were effected by Derby Works and all vehicles returned to traffic.

As a side note to this incident, while railway engineers were hard at work recovering the train and civil engineers were repairing the track, three young looters were caught robbing the buffet car while it was stabled in Hackney Yard adjacent to the accident scene.

The lines were reopened for normal working on 9 March 1997. ●

Left: *The recovery operation just about to get underway, with the Eastleigh tool vans arriving on site hauled by Class 37 No. 37895, but before the road cranes had been positioned.* CJM

Left Middle: *Detail of the destroyed axle head and bearing on TSO No. 42078.* CJM

Left Bottom: *Vehicles three to eight plus the rear power car, viewed from the side of the Teign Bridge before recovery commenced.* CJM

Below: *TSO No. 42078 which caused the accident came to rest straddling the middle girder of the River Teign bridge and could have easily toppled off during the final seconds of deceleration.* CJM

Above: *One of the major risks of a derailment such as Newton Abbot is vehicles toppling over, to reduce this risk vehicles are shored up with wood blocks, until the cranes are positioned to take the weight. Recovery engineers stand by to remove the supports as a South West Crane Hire heavy lift crane makes adjustment to its position in preparation to make a lift and reposition the vehicle on a siding track onto a pair of spare accommodation bogies. CJM*

Left: *Two South West Crane Hire cranes take the weight of the buffet car, while an engineer guides the vehicle to stop it swinging around. Frequently in derailments such as this vehicles part from their bogies or bogies are not usable due to damage and fresh accommodation bogies have to be provided. In this case the body was lifted and the third crane brought in was used to lift the bogies and position them on the siding track. CJM*

Modern Traction Rail Mishaps - A pictorial study

Above: *Passing over the top of the third crane which had been used to recover the bogies and had then lowered its jib, the buffet car is swung over the top of the crash site to be re-united with its wheelsets. When vehicles are lifted in this way, considerable care has to be exercised to ensure the recovery staff are not hit by falling objects or ballast off a lifted vehicle.* CJM

Right Middle & Bottom: *Engineers from Cardiff Canton, assisted by staff from Laira depot discuss the method of lifting of some of the TSO vehicles, which have badly twisted bogies dug into the ballast and will require a separate lift to remove them.* CJM

Pointwork Derailments

East Somerset Junction

At around 23.00 on Sunday 9 November 2008, multiple track circuit, signalling control and indication failures occurred in part of the area controlled by Westbury Power Box due to a power failure.

The failures affected the up and down Westbury lines around East Somerset Junction and the Merehead Quarry Branch.

At 00.25 partial power was restored but the branch remained affected. At 02.15 train 7A91 from Merehead to Acton, hauled by two Class 59/2s Nos. 59202 and 59204 with 43 loaded wagons giving a total train weight including locomotives of 4,505 tonnes left Merehead Quarry having been authorised by a Pilotman.

When setting the route at East Somerset Junction the signaller at Westbury forgot to set the points onto the up Westbury line, which meant that the catch point protecting the mainline remained open. As the train approached the junction he realised his mistake and placed a NRN broadcast. But the train was already approaching the points, the driver had already reduced his speed to 10.5mph (17km/h) and was looking to see what aspect the signal was displaying, when he saw that the points were not set correctly set and made an emergency brake application, but as the train was only 22 yards (20 m) from the point a derailment was inevitable. ■

Illustrations: Tony Bishop

Oxford

With a strong chance of toppling over from this angle, this was the position Class 50 No. 50004 *St Vincent* came to rest in late 1988 after a driver undertaking a run round move in Oxford Jericho Sidings continued on as far as Oxford North Junction and fell off the track on catch points.

Perhaps the drivers route knowledge was not up-to-date! ■

Illustration: Kevin Wills

In the autumn of 1978, Class 37/0 No. 37160 was running light loco off the Shireoaks line towards Doncaster Decoy via the curve at St Catherine's, when for some reason the train passed the signal protecting the junction and went through a pair of catch points.

The loco then toppled down the embankment and ended up on its side. Recovery was a complex operation requiring the use of two rail cranes, which lifted the damaged loco once ground stablisation had been undertaken.

The loco was then taken to BREL Doncaster Works for repair.

The view above shows how the loco

Potterick Carr

landed on its side, with a 'Fire Hazard' sign hanging on the front. The view below shows sister loco No. 37222 passing by on a grain train. ∎

Illustrations: Derek Porter

Inverurie

On 12 February 2004, the 06.25 Aberdeen to Inverness service formed of ScotRail-liveried Class 170 No. 17401, after arriving in the northbound platform at Inverurie a signal failure prevented the train from continuing towards the north.

After a southbound train had departed, it was agreed to set back the northbound train and route it over the southbound track through the station.

During this move the train became derailed, with the rear bogie of the rear coach taking the wrong line.

There was only minor damage to the train with no injuries to the 16 passengers and two crew on board.

Thankfully the train stopped where it did, as otherwise it would have demolished the semaphore signal. ■

Illustration: Owen Hodgson

Doncaster West Yard

A southbound EWS coal train taking the two way goods line through Doncaster on 23 July 2008 powered by Class 66/0 No. 66201 split the points at the north end of the station, with the leading bogie of the loco derailing.

The loco was rerailed with the aid of a road/rail tool and jacking van, but before normal working could be resumed some track repair work was required.

Note how the obstacle deflector plate on the loco has churned up the ballast. ■

Illustrations: Derek Porter

Fairwood Junction

The diamond crossover at Fairwood Junction south of Westbury, where the up Westbury avoiding line crossed over the down line from Westbury station used to have switched frogs.

On 5 April 1985, there appears to have been some sort of problem with the frogs, when Class 50 No. 50004 *St. Vincent* hauling the 10.27 Paddington to Paignton took a sharp right turn and started heading down the up main line in the wrong direction.

The driver brought the train to an immediate stand after the locomotive and five coaches had run over the crossover without derailing.

It was decided that the best course of action was to reverse the train back the way it had come. This it amazingly managed to do successfully and after an examination it continued its journey westward.

It is doubtful that in 2011 such quick remedial action of such an incident would have been made! ∎

Illustrations: John Chalcraft

Paignton

Just west of Paignton station is Goodrington Carriage Sidings, where some main line stock off arriving services recess before working departing trains. The sidings, fed by a single line from Paignton are protected by a catch point, to avoid the possibility of a head on collision with a train departing from the station from the 'up' line to the Torbay & Dartmouth Railway.

On 30 August 2007, then Virgin Cross Country-operated 'Super Voyage' Class 221 No. 221107 *Sir Martin Frobisher* forming a stock move from Goodrington Sidings to Paignton before departure for Newcastle, derailed approaching Sands Road level crossing Paignton, after the driver passed the protecting signal showing a stop aspect.

The set derailed just the leading bogie, and was re-railed later in the day using jacks and a transverser table, brought to the scene by road.

After an on site inspection, the set was moved under its own power to Plymouth Laira Depot for further assessment and return to traffic.

The view above shows the EWS re-railing crew getting ready to rerail the set, while the view left shows a Network Rail inspector making notes at the scene for the official enquiry. ■

Illustrations: Tony Christie

Marylebone

Over the years there have been literally hundreds of derailments involving Class 08 shunting locos, there can be few yards in the UK which has not been witness to some form of shunting mishap at some time.

On 10 June 1989, rail blue-liveried No. 08821 in use as the Marylebone station and yard pilot, derailed behind the signal box at Marylebone TMD.

As usual with the fixed wheelbase of the 0-6-0 shunter the loco ends up straddling the point work and can usually be rerailed by the use of jacks and a traversing table. ■

Illustration: Dave Rowland

Marine Colliery

Class 37/0 No. 37143 derailed and turned onto its side and went down an embankment at Marine Colliery, Ebbw Vale on 29 January 1975.

The derailment was caused by an incorrectly set of catch points, moved by the shunter in charge of the movement.

The locomotive was eventually recovered on 4 August 1975 using a specially constructed 'runway' of sleepers with winch ropes attached to a pulley. ■

Illustration: CJM Collection

Hatton

Friday 13 January 1978 was an unlucky day for BR in the Midlands, when Class 45/0 'Peak' No. 45042 derailed at the end of Hatton down loop while hauling a train of imported cars from Dover to Dorridge.

Recovery took place on Sunday 15 January 1978 with breakdown cranes from both Toton and Bescot working under a total possession. A large number of motor cars and motorcar flats were destroyed and the 'Peak' sustained serious damage to its No. 1 end. ■

Illustration: G. O Swain

Sideswipe Derailments

Hampton Court Junction

A lapse of concentration by the driver of the 13.13 Hampton Court to Waterloo on 23 February 1979 saw his train pass the protecting signal at Hampton Court Junction at danger and collide with the 12.20 Alton to Waterloo, hitting the train a glancing blow to its sixth coach.

The Hampton Court train formed of SUB sets 4662 and 4628 veered down the embankment with the leading and second coach in full derailment.

The Alton to Waterloo train formed of 4VEP No. 7708 and 4CIG No. 7423 continued unaware of the accident for some 840 yards, even though the rear bogie of the CIG parted from the train, leaving the carriage being dragged along the line.

Recovery was carried out by the Wimbledon Park-based crane and tool vans with the main lines reopening on 24 February and the Hampton Court branch on 26 February.

The sole reason for this accident was the passing of a signal at danger

The view above shows the SUB unit after recovery at Thames Ditton, the lower view shows the collision scene soon after the accident. ■

Illustrations: CJM

Bentley Colliery

It was very red faces for a pair of Doncaster drivers on 30 October 1980, when they ran around an MGR train at Bentley Colliery with two day old Class 56 No. 56084 and collided with the rear of their own train!

After recovery, the loco was taken directly back to BREL Doncaster for repair. ■
Illustration: CJM

Weymouth

More red faces for a loco crew and shunting staff, this time at Weymouth on 11 May 1963 when Class 04 No. D2295 was involved in a shunting mishap, when it set back into a rake of wagons already in the yard. ■
Illustration: Colin Caddy

Guildford

The 17.54 Waterloo to Portsmouth Harbour formed of 4 VEP No. 7741 and two 4 CIGs Nos. 7393 and 7407 were approaching Guildford on 19 August 1976.

The train was routed from the down main line to platform two. Standing in platform four, a continuation of the down main line, was an empty train formed of sets Nos. 7836 and 7815.

Due to a misunderstanding between the guard and driver of the train, it reversed out of the station against a red signal and collided with the rear of the Portsmouth Harbour train which was still crossing to the down main line. The last two coaches of the Portsmouth train and the leading coach of the empty stock train were derailed. Seven passengers were injured.

Car No. 76828 is illustrated, this was the coach on the Waterloo to Portsmouth train, which received serious side swipe damage. ■
Illustration: CJM

Railcar Repairs – Doncaster

From the 1960s through to the 1980s, Doncaster Works was the main Diesel Multiple Unit (DMU) collision repair facility for units operating on the Eastern and London Midland Regions. Collision and damage repairs shared classified overhaul space in the huge carriage repair shop at the north end of the works complex. ∎

Left: Taken inside the carriage repair building, after some of the damaged bodywork had been removed to allow the vehicle to be hauled to the site we see Lincoln-allocated Class 114 No. E56030, which sustained serious front end and side damage. Derek Porter

Below: Held together with a length of rope, Eastern Region allocated Class 108 DMC No. E50642 poses in the works yard on 2 October 1973 after receiving cab front damage. This vehicle received a new cab and roof and returned to the main line in around three months. Derek Porter

Modern Traction Rail Mishaps - A pictorial study

Right: The Metro-Cammell-built, later Class 101 fleet were usually represented at Doncaster Works, with such a large fleet size, it was common to find class members in need of attention. Taken on 9 June 1972, Eastern Region-allocated DTC No. E56364 awaits assessment with serious frontal damage on the drivers side which is documented to have been received in a level crossing accident. If the front end blind is anything to go by it may well have been working over the Marks Tey to Sudbury branch. Derek Porter

Below: Another Metro-Cammell Class 101 vehicle, this time No. 50190, a DMC vehicle from the London Midland Region-allocated stands at the back of the carriage works on 16 May 1973, with huge front end impact damage to the drivers side. Providing the main frame is sound, damage such as this could quickly be repaired with a new cab and roof fabricated in situ. Derek Porter

Sweet Hill Hassocks

19 December 1978

Stock:	Class 421 & 422 (CIG & BIG) EMUs, 7033, 7037, 7333, 7364, 7365
Train:	21.50 Victoria - Brighton & 21.40 Victoria - Littlehampton
Accident Type:	Rear end Collision
Passengers on train:	100
Fatalities:	3
Injuries:	20

A most destructive rear end collision occurred 506 yards (463m) north of Patcham Tunnel, below Sweet Hill Bridge on the main London to Brighton line at 23.22 on 19 December 1978.

Due to a passenger walking off the end of Brighton station, the third rail power supply had been discharged, and the 21.50 London Victoria to Brighton formed of CIG No. 7364, BIG No. 7033 and CIG No. 7333, was brought to a stand close to Patcham Tunnel, the rear of the train was below Sweet Hill bridge.

After being stationary for around two minutes, the train was slammed into at between 45-50mph (72-80km/h) by the following 21.40 London Victoria to Littlehampton train formed of CIG No. 7365 and BIG No. 7037.

The impact was so severe, that the rear (coach 12) of the front train was deflected to the right, while coach 11 was tossed into the air, with the leading coach of impacting train passing under the vehicle and crashing into and under the 10th vehicle. The severity of the impact damaged every coach of the two trains in some way.

Being late in the evening, the passenger figures on both trains was very low and this certainly kept the injuries and death toll to a very low figure considering the damage.

The accident was investigated by Major C. F. Rose, who found the two main causes. One, that the red signal that should have been protecting the stationary train was not displaying any aspect at all, and thus offered no indication of the trains presence ahead. Secondly the driver of the 21.40 Victoria to Littlehampton made no effort to reduce the speed of his train on passing the previous signal, which was confirmed to have been showing a single yellow aspect. Why this was the case could not be proven, as sadly the driver lost his life in the accident.

The report concludes that had the BR Automatic Warning System (AWS) been in use

on the line and trains at the time, it was very likely that the accident would have been averted, as the driver would have had the restrictive aspect of the yellow signal drawn to his attention.

Recovery was a major operation, with great difficulty in parting the tangled remains under

Sweet Hill bridge. The presence of asbestos was also a major consideration during recovery work.

The line between Heywards Heath and Brighton did not return to normal operation until 23 December. CIG units 7333 and 7365 were written off following this accident. ●

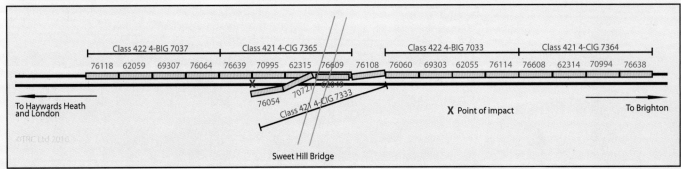

Left, Above and Below: *Three views of the devastation at Sweet Hill Bridge, taken the day following the accident. It is hard to imagine the force generated by this impact to virtually destroy five Mk1 design vehicles. The presence of the bridge obviously helped in compressing the vehicles. Recovery was made with the use of both road and rail cranes, with some vehicles being broken up on site. Note the plastic signs hanging on the safety cordon warning of the presence of asbestos and some of the rescue staff wearing breathing apparatus. The image below shows what was the rear end of the front train.* CJM Collection

Unusual Incidents

Washwood Heath

The products of the Land Rover assembly plant in the West Midlands used to be loaded onto rail flats in Washwood Heath yard.

This bizarre incident occurred on 27 February 1995 when an articulated rail wagon parted company during shunting leaving this Range Rover perched between the two wagon sections. ■

Illustration: Phil Cotterhill

Jarrow Yard

During a shunting move in Jarrow Yard on 15 October 1984 one set back move went just a tad too far, with a ZTO BR standard brake van being forced over the top of the buffer stops.

The impact removed the buffer heads, demolished the buffer stops which then acted as a launch pad for the brake van, which lost its wheels and underframe equipment. ■

Illustration: L. Abram

London Bridge

On 16 November 1970, an incoming train into the South Central side of London Bridge very nearly arrived on the platform rather than the track!

Ex-works 2HAP No. 6167 on the rear of a train, split the points with the rear coach No. 76015 ending up part on the platform and part on the track, it is quite amazing how the coach did not turn over. ■
Illustration: CJM Collection

Clapham Junction

Accidents do not always involve trains, such as this incident on 11 May 1965 when Clapham Junction 'A' signal box started to fall down while trains were running.

The Nine Elms crane was called and held up the structure while repairs were carried out. ■
Illustration: P. J. Gillmor

Driver Error

Eltham Well Hall

A railway staff day out to Margate from Cricklewood turned into disaster on 11 June 1972, when the returning train, powered by Class 47/0 No. D1630 crashed at speed at Eltham Well Hall, after taking the 20mph (32km/h) curve at 65mph (105km/h).

It is sad to report that the driver of the train, based at Hither Green had been drinking heavily during the day before signing on duty by telephone, and later with his secondman continued drinking in the railway staff association club in Ramsgate.

The subsequent public inquiry found the sole cause of the accident was the driver being in a drunk condition.

The loco and all but one of its 10 Mk1 carriages derailed. The driver lost his life, as did five passengers. 126 other passengers were injured.

Amazingly when looking at the above picture, No. D1630 was rebuilt by BREL Crewe and returned to traffic as 47048 and was eventually rebuilt as 47570 and 47849. ■
Illustration: CJM

York Skelton

Driver error was blamed for a serious accident which occurred at York Skelton on 24 July 1994, when Class 47/7 No. 47743 *The Bobby* powering the 17.42 Bristol to Low Fell Royal Mail service.

After departing from York, the train traversed the slow line and derailed on catch points close to the River Ouse bridge near Skelton Junction. The loco turned over on its side and rolled down a 30ft (9.1m) embankment trapping the driver in his cab for more than five hours. Eventually the driver had to have his leg amputated to extract him from the wreckage.

The Class 47 was not rescued from the scene, but broken up on site in October 1995.
Illustration: Richard Lillie

Glanrhyd

On Monday 19 October 1987, the 05.27 Swansea to Shrewsbury service was formed of a Class 108 DMMU consisting of DMS No. 52037 leading, and DMBS No. 51910 trailing.

The South West Wales area had been subjected to extreme flooding due to an exceptionally heavy rainfall over a period of 27 hours starting late on the preceding Saturday night.

The Glary Bridge is a single-track structure crossing the River Towy between Landfill and Langdon on the Central Wales line. Due to the original wrought iron girders becoming overstressed the bridge was reconstructed in 1958, it also carried a public footbridge on it's downstream side.

Late on the Sunday evening, the driver of a light engine returning southbound from Craven Arms reported to the signalman at Pantyffynon that he had passed three areas of flooding on the line with ballast washed away in one location. He had also stopped on the Glanrhyd river bridge and judged that the water level was approximately three feet below the level of the decking and felt that the bridge structure was sound.

The signalman passed the flooding report to the on-call Traffic Manager who drove to the area to try and check the situation, but owing to the darkness and flooded roads he was unable to carry out a full assessment.

It was therefore decided to use the 05.27 Shrewsbury service to carry out a check of

line the following morning.

The floodwater cascading down the River Towy was scouring the base supports of the bridge and at some point in the early hours of Monday morning bridge pier No. 3 gave way under the weight of the structure with insufficient material left in its base.

The train had left Llandeilo at 07.05 with six passengers, the driver and guard plus two members of railway staff one of whom was the Permanent Way Section Supervisor who were present to check the line. About five minutes after leaving Llandeilo the train ran onto the Glanrhyd bridge at a speed of between 10-15 mph (16-24km/h) there was then a loud cracking noise and the front coach fell into the river at an angle to the rear coach which remained upright and

on the bridge. The two coaches remained connected for a while although at an angle, which was allowing the flood water to rush through the gap, but some of the occupants of the front coach managed to get through to the safety of the rear coach. Eventually the front coach broke free and dropped completely into the water.

Sadly three passengers and the train driver were trapped inside the coach and drowned.

The line remained closed for just over a year while a new bridge was built re-opening on 30 October 1988. For the duration of the blockage, the public service had been maintained by a bus link between Llandeilo and Llangadog. ■

Illustrations: Tom Clift

Head on Collisions

Bellgrove

In April 1987 the double junction at Bellgrove which is just over a mile east of Glasgow Queen Street on the Helensburgh to Airdrie surburban line was converted to a single lead junction with a line speed of 30mph (48km/h).

This single lead was the scene of a head on collision at 12.47 on 6 March 1989. The trains involved were the 12.39 Springburn to Milngavie formed of Class 303 three-car EMU No. 303005 and the 12.20 Milngavie to Springburn formed of Class 303 set No. 303071.

A driver and one passenger were killed travelling in the train from Springburn, the driver of the other train was seriously injured. 54 passengers were taken to hospital all but five were released on the same day.

The enquiry into the accident concluded that it was caused by the driver of the train from Milngavie departing from Bellgrove station and passing a signal at danger protecting the junction. ■

Illustration: Tom Noble

Lenton

Just before dawn on 16 December 1971 a major accident occurred at Lenton Junction, Nottingham, when a southbound coal train from Bestwood Park to Derby was struck head on by the 01.30 Liverpool to Nottingham parcels.

The coal train was powered by two Type 1s Nos. D8115 and D8142, while the parcels was headed by Type 2 No. D7605.

The impact was such that the Type 2 was totally destroyed, while the leading cab of the Type 1 was crushed, sadly both drivers and the guard of the parcels train were killed. The view below shows recovery getting under-way.

The official findings into the accident placed the blame on the driver of the parcels train for missing a red signal. ■

Illustration: Jack Hooke

Colwich

Colwich Junction is where the Manchester route via Stone diverges from the West Coast Main Line. The track formation from the London direction consists of, down fast, down slow; up fast and up slow with both routes becoming double track after the junction.

There is also a crossover 259 yards (237m) prior to the diamond crossing from the down slow to the down fast. A train travelling to Manchester on the down fast has to first cross over onto the down slow line, it then crosses the up fast line on a switched diamond crossing.

On 17 August 1986 the signalling at the junction was altered to enable the crossover from the down fast to down slow to be traversed at 50mph (80km/h). This was achieved by the use of flashing yellow aspects on the approach signals.

If the route ahead was clear it would show a single yellow and would change on approach release to whatever aspect was allowed by the signalling ahead which was the signal at the crossover from the down slow to down fast and was 259 yards (237m) prior to the diamond crossing.

Prior to this change there would have been a single yellow prior to the signal at the crossover from the down fast to down slow which would show a red aspect until approach released.

On the day of the accident, 19 September 1986, two trains were approaching Colwich Junction from opposite directions. The 17.00 Euston to Manchester which took the route via Stone hauled by Class 86/4 No. 86429 *The Times* with 13 coaches and the 17.20 Liverpool Lime Street to Euston hauled by Class 86/2 No. 86211 *City of Milton Keynes* with 12 coaches.

The driver of the Euston to Manchester train believed that the flashing yellow signals meant that his route was clear over the junction. As he approached the red signal at the crossover from the down slow to the down fast he believed that it was approach controlled and would change to a proceed aspect. By the time he realised the signal was not going to change, and even after making an emergency brake application the train continued towards the junction.

The Liverpool to Euston train was under clear signals and travelling at between 90 and 100mph (144-161km/h) and had no time to stop when he saw the other train. The two struck virtually head on, by now the northbound train had almost come to a stand on the crossing.

The driver of the Liverpool train was killed instantly; the driver of the Manchester train along with a person who was travelling in the cab with him jumped clear at the last second and although both were showered with debris were relatively unhurt.

Of the 873 passengers on the trains 75 were injured.

Both locomotives were written off along with three Mk2, two Mk3 and one Mk1 coaches, some having to be cut up on site along with another four coaches having extensive damage requiring major repairs.

The enquiry found that the accident was caused by the lack of knowledge of the driver of the Euston to Manchester train of the revised signalling at the junction. Even though he had signed the relevant notice regarding the change he admitted that he had not actually read it. ■

Illustrations: Top: Gary S. Smith
Middle & Bottom: Andy Fudge

Repair Time

A number of major repair sites have operated over the years throughout the UK rail network, these have ranged from BR operated repair facilities to the private sector who offer specialist collision and damage repair services.

The British Rail Engineering Ltd (BREL) factories operated a major collision repair service, but following privatisation and the sale to Bombardier less of this type of work is undertaken. Private companies such as Brush Traction and the Bombardier sites at Crewe and Derby offer the main repair services. ■

Left Top: *The BREL facility at Derby Litchurch Lane, long associated with building coaching stock and multiple units also operated a major vehicle repair function, this has been continued under privatisation firstly with ABB and currently with Bombardier. Here a Class 310 EMU driving car No. 76158 receives a new front end following a rear end collision. The view was recorded at Derby Litchurch Lane on 13 March 1995. CJM*

Left Middle: *Damaged in an accident at Skipton on 22 January 1992 when it was run into by Class 144 No. 144017, Class 37 No. 37681 was recovered first to Doncaster Works for assessment and then transferred to ABB Crewe Works where this picture was recorded on 27 April 1995. The loco was broken up in August 1995. CJM*

Below: *In ABB Transportation days, Derby Litchurch Lane was the main EMU repair facility. On 11 March 1993, a Driving Motor Standard from set No. 315828 nears completion after a section of the driving cab had been replaced following impact damage. New head, marker and tail lights were still awaited as well as handrails before a full repaint into NSE colours. CJM*

Above: *The last slam door vehicle to receive a new fabricated front end was vehicle 76024 from Class 421 set No. 1710. This followed collision damage, with the DTC vehicle having a new front end specially assembled at Derby Litchurch Lane, a massive undertaking considering the life expectancy for the fleet was so short. Recorded at Derby Litchurch Lane on 11 September 1996. CJM*

Below: *ABB Derby Litchurch Lane also undertook a number of aluminium body repairs, on the more modern passenger fleet. In this view recorded on 11 September 1996 driving car No. 58881 from Class 165 No. 165120 receives a new front end, after having front end and cab side damage. CJM*

Above: A depot side swipe at Wimbledon required DTS No. 77743 from Class 455/7 No. 5709 to have major bodyside repairs in August 1994. The impact by the first door opening was a difficult repair with the entire area cut out and new material inserted. The coach is seen here at ABB Derby Litchurch soon after arrival while an assessment of repairs was being undertaken. CJM

Left Middle: HST Trailer First No. 41043 operated by Great North Eastern Railway was involved in a depot accident in 2006 and transferred to Brush Traction for inspection and assessment of work needed. After a long time in the shop, it was decided not to repair the coach and it was later transferred to Wabtec Doncaster. In 2010 it was agreed the coach should be repaired with the complex operation being undertaken at Wabtec Doncaster. This view of the vehicle was recorded on 6 July 1006 at Brush Traction, Loughborough. CJM

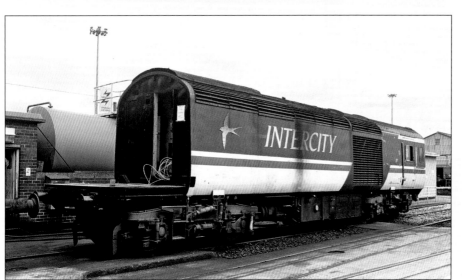

Left Below: Following its collision at Newton Abbot on 25 March 1994, when it was run into by a Class 158, Class 43 power car No. 43071 was taken to ABB Crewe for assessment and repair. A complete new cab was required which took many months to order and install. In this view, recorded in the works yard on 17 July 1995 the vehicle has received underframe repairs and was awaiting admission to the main shop for a new cab assembly to be installed. CJM

Modern Traction Rail Mishaps - A pictorial study

Above and Below: *ABB Crewe undertook a number of significant loco repairs, including a number of Class 37s when these were still prime motive power for both the freight and passenger sectors. An accident in Cornwall in 1994 involved Class 37/4 No. 37411 and Class 37/6 No. 37669. Both locos required new nose sections. No. 37411 is seen in the above view with staff dealing with the frame just above the buffer beam as part of the straightening process. In the view below No. 37669 is seen after stripping and cutting away the damaged buffer beam before repair work started. Note that both locos carry the St Blazey depot logo on the secondmans cab side. Both locos are painted in Railfreight Distribution livery. Both: CJM*

In todays privatised railway, Network Rail are responsible for the recovery of derailment and accident scenes, with breakdown trains operated by DBS.

Three 75 tonne lift capacity Cowans Sheldon diesel hydraulic cranes are available 24 hours a day seven days a week and can be quickly taken to any accident scene. However today, a greater use of road based high-capacity cranes is made.

The Toton allocated crane No. ADRC96715 is seen at Taunton, with its runner wagons uncoupled and its jib retracted. ∎
Illustration: Brian Garrett

In the quest for efficiency a number of road-rail recovery equipment vehicles are available.

These vehicles can operate on the highway using normal rubber tyres or can when required be positioned over railway tracks and lower rail wheels for operation over the rail network. These vehicles can operate to accident scenes and if needed haul one or two light weight rail vehicles, as demonstrated in this picture showing a BRUFF vehicle at Morpeth hauling a NKA Royal Mail wagon following an accident involving Class 47 No. 47783. ∎
Illustration: Ian S. Carr

A M&EE Department BRUFF vehicle showing its integral turntable lifting the vehicle for rail mounting or direction turning. The weight of the vehicle is taken by a scissor lift. The vehicles are based on a Bedford 7.5 or 8.5 tonne road chassis and use 300mm diameter rail wheels. ■
Illustration: CJM

Network Rail in Scotland have recently been using this Iveco road truck to attend accident and derailment scenes. Registered in November 2005 it is painted in day-glow orange with staff and equipment access through a forward door of the hood section. ■
Illustration: Donald Stirling

In the days when a number of small wheelbase 4-wheel wagons were in traffic, most depots which had a crane allocated also had one or more 'Weltrol' wagons on their books, which could easily carry a wagon from a derailment site back to a yard or depot. The 1970s Wimbledon based well wagon No. ADB900911, built at Swindon, is seen at Wimbledon West Yard in 1974 carrying 16 ton Coal wagon No. B555730. This wagon had been involved in a derailment at Merton Abbey and was declared unfit for movement by rail. ■
Illustration: CJM

Ransomes & Rapier 45 ton lift capacity steam crane No. DS81 was allocated to Ashford Chart Leacon for many years, it was later renumbered into the national system as ADRR95201 and is now preserved at the Kent & East Sussex Railway.

During its time based at Ashford, the crane with its runners and staff and tool vans was on call for the Southern Region South Eastern Division and was made available to assist any other area if required.

In the mid 1970s the crane was displayed at an Ashford Chart Leacon open day and is seen outside the inspection shed giving a lifting demonstration.

Behind the crane is a Class 71 'booster' electric which was used on the South Eastern Division on both passenger and freight duties. ■

Illustration: CJM

In the 1960s and 70s the Southern Region of BR operated two 75 ton lift capacity diesel-electric cranes, one was based at Ashford No. ARDC96200 and the other ARDC96201 was allocated to Wimbledon Park.

Both were built by Cowans Sheldon of Carlisle and were originally painted in red, in the 1980s high visibility yellow was applied.

The crane vehicle was mounted on an eight wheel chassis, with escort and jib runners making up a sizeable train. The crane usually operated with two or three staff and tool vans.

The crane is seen here in action in Woking up yard, recovering derailed ballast wagons. Note the staff member on the ground watching the operation of the crane. ■

Illustration: CJM

A pair of 75 tonne lift capacity diesel cranes, No. ARDC96706 from Toton being nearest the camera, perform a tandem lift of Mk2 TSO No. M5535 at Dorridge on 1 October 1984 following a derailment on 30 September of the 11.40 Manchester Piccadilly to Brighton. ■
Illustration: Chris Morrison

The Toton-allocated 36 ton lift capacity steam crane No. ARDC95223 is seen hard at work at Branston Junction, south of Burton-on-Trent on 16 May 1984. The crane is rerailing Class 56 No. 56067.

This crane, built by Cowans Sheldon was originally numbered RS1106/45 and had a 45 tonne lift capacity. ■
Illustration: John Tuffs

Modern Traction Rail Mishaps - A pictorial study

Ransomes & Rapier crane No. ADRR95201 was built with a 45 tonne lift capacity but this was reduced in the 1980s to 36 tonne capacity. After working at Ashford Chart Leacon for many years, the crane transferred to Stewarts Lane, where this illustration of the vehicle was taken on 22 September 1985 when it was being prepared for a lifting job. On the right is a water tanker No. ADB998990, while on the far left is depot pilot loco No. 08837. ■
Illustration: CJM

Breakdown cranes are not always used for accident recovery work and when more depots had such a tool available were frequently used to lift locomotives to allow bogie or traction motor changes, especially if the depots jacks were out of use or being used for another job.

Taken at Aberdeen Ferryhill depot in Scotland on 21 March 1974, the depot crane lifts a traction motor into a bogie frame, while Class 06 0-4-0 Barclay No. 2423 stands attached. ■
Illustration: Brian Morrison

Old Dalby

The most spectacular deliberate rail crash in the UK was staged at the BR Research test track at Old Dalby on behalf of the Central Electricity Generating Board (CEGB), when a three-coach loco-hauled passenger train was crashed at 100mph (161km/h) into a nuclear flask wagon to prove its integrity. The crash took place on 17 July 1984.

The collision was staged as a public demonstration to dispel fears that a nuclear waste flask could not survive the impact of a rail crash. Needless to say the flask survived intact unlike the locomotive.

Two redundant Class 46 'Peak' locos were allocated to the test, Nos. 46009 and 46023. No. 46009 was used on the crash run, with No. 46023 together with three Mk1s kept in reserve.

On the day of the crash, No. 46009 with Mk1 coaches Nos. 25154, 4514 and 26654 were set off from the northern end of the Old Dalby test track with the driving controls set and no-one in the cab.

This was achieved by fitting an extra brake isolating cock on the sole bar of the loco near to the cab footsteps. Once everything was set in the cab, the power controller was opened and the driver got out, closing the brake isolating cock from

the ground.

The site chosen for the crash was just south of the Old Dalby control centre, where the main test track was cut and slewed across into the old headshunt of the former Army base exchange sidings.

Viewing grandstands were erected for the invited guests and members of the press (The author being one) and the area was equipped with heavy security fencing and patrolled by guards.

The 'Peak' with its three coaches accelerated towards the flask, gaining speed to 100mph (161km/h) and slammed into pre-positioned derailed flask wagon No. B55019 which contained one standard cube flask.

The locomotive broke its back on impact with the flask, tossed the wagon in the air (clearly visible in the image bottom left), and came to a stop in little more than the length of the train.

While the locomotive was destroyed and it is without doubt any crew on board would have been killed, the flask showed little damage after its impact and there would have been no leak of its contents. The robustness of the flask wagon was also shown, with the near intact wagon landing smashed into the inner end of the first coach.

In the upper view the flask can be seen at the far end of the second coach.

No. 46009 and the three coaches were later cut up on site by Vic Berry of Leicester.

The spare train, powered by No. 46023 was formed of vehicles Nos. 25038, 7940 and 25447. ■

Illustrations: Left: CJM, Above: John Tuffs, Right Middle and Right Bottom: CJM

Old Oak Common

Training in different methods of vehicle recovery is very important to the recovery teams and sometimes when new or revised technologies are introduced, full scale training exercises are arranged.

One such event was staged at Old Oak Common depot in West London in November 1972.

To demonstrate new air bag vehicle righting equipment, withdrawn 'Hymek' No. D7100 was turned onto its side with the aid of the Old Oak Common crane and then righted using air bags. Several demonstrations of the equipment were made.

The exercise did lift the loco upright but rendered some serious dents in the bodyside.

The loco was eventually taken to Swindon for scrapping in February 1974. ■

Illustrations: CJM

Modern Traction Rail Mishaps - A pictorial study

Temple Mills

A similar rerailing exercise as to the one illustrated at Old Oak Common on the opposite page was staged at Temple Mills in 1971, when an oil wagon was turned over and rerailed, or more accurately returned to an upright position by the use of inflated air bags. ∎
Illustration: CJM

Dawlish

A very important part of railway safety and the guarantee that passengers and staff can be rescued from a train crash scene as quickly as possible is ongoing training of railway staff and the emergency services.

Frequent 'desk top' training exercises are held with members of rail staff with fire, police and ambulance personnel, ensuring the front line first responders to any accident have knowledge to gain access to a train and work safely within a rail environment.

In addition to 'desk top' exercises, a number of train crash scenarios are held with real trains each year, these might be in sidings, depots or on the main line. Frequently the railway and the rescue authorities arrange these events without the knowledge of front line personnel who will respond and think it is an actual accident scene. Monitors gauge the staffs performance and then debrief sessions follow ensuring as much as possible can be learnt from the valuable training.

One such accident exercise was held on 9 October 1994 inside Kennaway and Coryton Tunnels, just west of Dawlish station, when a westbound HST 'crashed' and the emergency services attended. A number of casualties were made up to represent wounded and some people played 'dead' to gauge the response from rescue teams. A triage centre was set up in a local street and casualties were removed from the train in much the same way as a real accident.

A considerable amount was learnt from local responders from this exercise for which the editor played a member of the press trying to get on site. ∎
Illustration: CJM

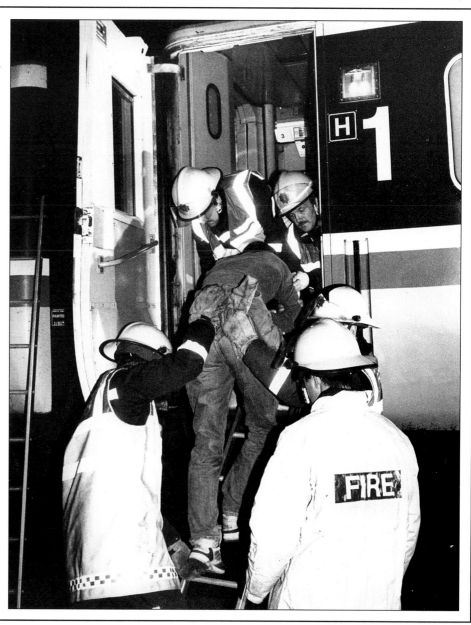

Location Index

Modern Traction Rail Mishaps - A pictorial study